A CHILD OF GOD I AM, AMEN!

Scriptures, Confessions, and Prayers for Children

Pam Reece

Book Design by HMDpublishing

"Behold, I and the children whom the LORD hath
given me are for signs and for wonders..."
Isaiah 8:18 (KJV)

CONTENTS

ACKNOWLEDGEMENT

I want to give a special shoutout to my amazing family and close friends (there are too many to name individually) who have been my unwavering support system. They have prayed for me, lifted me, given me endless encouragement, and have never allowed me to give up.

Special recognition to:

My mentor: Dr. Kishma George, Instagram @drkishmageorge

Professional photo by: Jackie Hicks, Instagram @fondmemories!

Professional make-up by: Letitia Thornhill, Instagram @letbeautyl

DEDICATION

I express my gratitude to the Lord Jesus Christ, who summoned and appointed me before the world's foundations, empowering me to live out His God-ordained plan for my life. My purpose encompasses healing, liberation, empowerment, impartation, and leaving an enduring influence on individuals' lives, all to glorify Him. It is a humbling and awe-inspiring experience to be selected as part of God's intricate plan and divine intentions.

I am who I am by God's grace and mercy.

To You, Oh Lord, I dedicate this book.

This message is for all the parents, including mothers, fathers, aunts, uncles, siblings, foster parents, spiritual parents, stepparents, "step-up/step-in" parents, godparents, adopted parents, and grandparents. If you are purchasing this book as a gift or for your home, may it serve as a valuable resource to inspire and guide you in raising your children to revere God. May it teach them to love God with all their hearts and make His Word the foundation of their lives despite attempts by different systems, activists, or governments to redefine, implement, or enforce ideologies. God's Word is powerful and true. As God Himself said, "Children are a wonderful gift from the Lord, and their existence is a testament to His blessings." (Psalms 127:3)

They shall multiply and flourish, as numerous as the stars in the sky and the sand on the seashore, destined to overcome any challenges that may arise. (Genesis 22:17, ICB).

Arise and take your place, parents! God is holding you accountable. Raise your Godly seed!

Then the people brought their little children to Jesus
so he could put his hands on them and pray for them.
His followers told them to stop, but Jesus said, "Let the
little children come to me. Don't stop them, because the
kingdom of heaven belongs to people who are like these
children."After Jesus put his hands on the children, he
left there. Matthew 19:13-15, (NCV)

RAISING GODLY SEED

"Children are a gift from the Lord; they are a reward from Him. Children born to a young man are like arrows in a warrior's hands. How joyful is the man whose quiver is full of them! He will not be put to shame when he confronts his accusers at the city gates." (Psalms 127)

Children are our hope for today and for a brighter future. They are a heritage from the Lord. One of the purposes of marriage is for procreation (production of offspring) -- the perpetuation of Godly generations ~ children that are taught of the Lord ~ to love, honor, and glorify Him. Godly parents guide, train, and lead their children to love and reverence God. One of the main reasons God called and chose Abraham is because He knew Abraham ensured that God's Word and promises would be disseminated throughout the generations. "Then God said, "Shall I keep back from Abraham what I'm about to do? Abraham will become a large and strong nation; all the world's nations will find themselves blessed through him. Yes, I've settled on him as the one to train his children and future family to observe God's way of life, live kindly, generously, and fairly, so that God can complete in Abraham what he promised him." (Genesis 18:17-19, The Message Bible)

The scriptures clearly instruct us to "train a child in the way he should go, and when he is old, he will not depart." (Proverbs 22:6) That scripture alone, if believed and applied ~ guarantees that even if your child takes a different (unapproved) direction, the child will repent (change their mind) and return to the right path. God also instructs us to "bring them up in the training and admonition of the Lord." This isn't optional -- it's a mandate given by God. Also, it doesn't mean to raise children to be afraid of God but to honor, love, trust, and worship God for everything concerning them. We want to create an awareness of the truth of God because He is indeed the only true and living God. We are to teach our children to lean on and trust God for help and direction concerning choices and decisions for their future. A Word of God-based pursuit never ends in calamity! God's word is "spirit and life." God's word is our authority, our foundation on which we build upon. When we trust and follow God's way of doing things, the outcome is always for our lifting.

Thank you for choosing this book to help teach and train your children in the Word of God. The miracle of bringing a child into the world will forever remain astounding. While we are overloaded with information on parenthood, as children of God who have established that the Word of God is our only foundation and authority, it is of utmost importance that we uphold, speak, declare, defend, and decree the Word of God over every aspect of our lives, and that includes our children. The Word of God will instill reverence, guidance, truth, love, confidence, security, and acceptance in our children. While the moral fabric of nations is deteriorating with the intent to steal, kill, and destroy, God's Word will never fade, fail, or fall short of its purpose and promises. God's Word is Spirit (God-breathed), and His Word is Life (God's very being and essence), John 6:63.

The Word will always retain its effectiveness, power, and efficacy. God's Word is full of fervent power and is ever available, active, and able. However, if you don't know the Word of God -- if you don't activate it -- if you don't engage or utilize the Sword of the Spirit (Ephesians 6:17), you and your children will be subject to failure, shame, disgrace, and even worse, tragedy.

We are admonished to "train up a child," so when they have graduated to being independent ~ whether it be off to college/

university, or to reside in other parts of the country and the world, start their businesses or careers, get married and start their own families -- the Word that was established while under your care, will rise and cause them to remember what God has said – no matter the circumstances. The Word of God instilled and solidified by constant memorization, meditation application, prayer, recall, and practice will frame their conscience. The Word of God, established (applied or practiced regularly), will assist your children in decisions, regardless of the latest trends and society's beliefs. The Word of God will rise within them to make the right choices.

Please note, no matter how old your child is – whether an infant or a grown adult, you are still their spiritual custodian. As a parent, you have an obligation and a responsibility to teach, practice, and instill the scriptures and to continually (unceasingly) pray for them. Suppose your children are now adults, and you didn't have a relationship with God and didn't establish God's Word in their lives when they were young? Is it too late? NO, IT'S NOT LATE! God's abundant mercies endure forever! So, begin where you are right now! Pray for them with prayer points backed by the Word of God. Build an altar of prayer in your home. Take your children's pictures to your prayer altar and constantly remind God of what He has said concerning your children. Your prayers based on God's Word are powerful and effective. God's power and love are potent enough to reach and deliver your adult children wherever they are. So, pray consistently for them and never, ever give up! Teach your children to go to God through prayer and the Word so they don't resort to the world!

Below are scriptures that support the overall theme of this book. Please note this isn't an all-inclusive reference tool but a foundation you can build upon.

I encourage you to read, meditate, and memorize them repeatedly. Then, go through every scripture and confession with your child. Make it a point to do it every day, whether before school, at family worship, or at night before bedtime. Eventually, you'll see that the Word will take root and begin to manifest and produce itself. The Word that's been meditated, memorized, and applied is the Word that will take residence on the inside of your children and have proof.

Your child can outgrow this book, but they will never outgrow God's word. So, get more scriptures for them! Meditate, memorize, and apply them continually. And, when you think you've got all the scriptures here, go back and do it again. Why? Because God's Word is life. It'll answer for today's needs, and those same scriptures will speak to their tomorrow and future. Your involvement in your child's spiritual growth is crucial today. Raising children these days necessitates establishing a firm grounding in God's Word. Without this strong foundation, they become susceptible to deception, lust, and perversion influences.

You can't bring children into the world and raise them without a solid foundation of God's word and expect them not to be affected by spirits of deception, lust, and perversion. The world has changed drastically! Let's go back to the Bible! Nowhere in the world is there any literary work that has the power to speak life, heal, deliver, affirm, and set free. God's word builds up, edifies, calms doubt, and dispels fears and insecurity. God's word heals, delivers, prospers, makes whole, provides wisdom and instruction, helps, provides everlasting freedom, and establishes faith. God's word will also rebuke, warn, correct, and instruct! Oh yes, but only because error, sin, or ignorance are present. What loving parents would let their children get away with anything terrible and not correct them? Because your child requires Bible-based teaching, you wouldn't provide worldly teaching. You wouldn't project a Godly lifestyle at home and then turn it off when you're with your friends. After all, children learn what they live. So, stay the course....and maintain the process. Remain steadfast. It shows you have faith, and faith pleases God. Hebrews 11:6. Your faithful stewardship over your children will pay off if you are consistent.

Parents, you must make room for God by eliminating as many distractions as possible. So, turn off the television. Put away the smart devices and pick up a hard copy of the BIBLE. Teach your children the books of the Old and the New Testaments. Show them how to find the accounts of Creation, the Ten Commandments, the faith of Abraham and Sarah, David's victory over Goliath, the Birth of Jesus Christ, and so much more. Have family devotions and teach your children to pray for children worldwide; teach them to repent and ask for forgiveness for their wrongdoings; teach them to worship God through praise, worship, and prayers.

Before I Go Any Further, Look at This Alarming Story:

The 6-year-old boy who seriously wounded his teacher at a Virginia elementary school in January (2023) said in the aftermath that "I did it" and "I got my mom's gun last night," according to newly unsealed court documents.

The child made the statements to another teacher who had restrained him after he opened fire on his first-grade teacher, Abigail Zwerner, as she sat reading to her class at Richneck Elementary School in Newport News, according to a probable cause statement and search warrant affidavit.

The documents shed light on how the boy likely obtained the 9 mm semi-automatic handgun, used in the shooting. His mother, Deja Taylor, told Newport News police in an interview that she typically "stores her firearm in her purse with a trigger lock in place, or a lock box," according to the probable cause statement.

On Jan. 6, the morning of the shooting, Taylor believed the gun was in her purse with the trigger lock installed and left on top of her bedroom dresser, according to the statement. She added that the key for the lock is kept under her bedroom mattress.

Newport News police have previously said the gun was legally purchased but were investigating whether it was secured correctly, as claimed by the child's family.

James Ellenson, a lawyer for the family, has said Taylor believes the gun was placed on a high closet shelf with a trigger lock. But he acknowledged in May that questions remain about how the child accessed the weapon.

"People have talked to him about that, but I don't know that any adult knows exactly how he got the gun," Ellenson told ABC News.

As part of the investigation, Taylor, 26, pleaded guilty in federal court in June to the use of marijuana while possessing a firearm. She is expected to be sentenced in October and could receive 18 to 24 months in prison.

Federal prosecutors said the narcotics were discovered during a court-ordered home search in connection with the shooting at Richneck Elementary School. It is illegal to use marijuana while possessing a firearm under U.S. law.

"A search of Taylor's phone revealed numerous text messages illustrating the pervasive scope of Taylor's marijuana use," according to prosecutors. Meanwhile, "a lockbox was not found in either of the residences nor was a trigger lock or key to a trigger lock ever found."

Taylor faces separate state charges related to the shooting of felony child neglect and a misdemeanor count of recklessly leaving a loaded firearm to endanger a child. A plea hearing in the case is scheduled for Aug. 15.

The 6-year-old's ability to retrieve the gun and then use it on a teacher at his elementary school is at the heart of a case that brought national attention to school safety and stunned the community when police announced the child's actions appeared intentional.

The child's family has previously said he suffers from an "acute disability" and received the "treatment he needs" under a court-ordered temporary detention at a medical facility.

As part of a care plan at the school, officials said the boy's parents were supposed to be with him daily but were absent on the day of the shooting.

The unsealed court documents say police arrived at the classroom to find the gun and cartridge casings lying on the floor. School staff members were aiding Zwerner, who was shot in her left hand and upper chest.

Another teacher told police that the children had returned from recess when she heard a gunshot as she walked by. Children fled from the classroom, followed by an injured Zwerner. The teacher went in and saw the 6-year-old standing by his desk, and she held him until police arrived, according to the documents.

When the teacher told police, the boy was making statements, including, "I shot that b---- dead," the documents said.

In response to the release of the documents this week, Ellenson reiterated that the child has "severe emotional issues."

"He is in therapy and improving daily. We wish to thank the dedicated professionals working with him," he said in an email.

A local prosecutor said in March that the 6-year-old would not face charges given that a young child wouldn't have the competency to understand the legal system or adequately assist an attorney. Lawyers for Zwerner have said that claims made by the family that the gun was safely secured at home "defied common sense."

In April, Zwerner filed a $40 million lawsuit alleging school administrators shrugged off multiple warnings from staff and students who believed the boy had a gun and posed an imminent threat on the day of the shooting and did so knowing the child "had a history of random violence."

The Newport News School Board has argued that the suit should be dismissed and that the case should go before the Virginia Workers' Compensation Commission because Zwerner's injuries occurred on the job.

A judge ruled last month that lawyers for Zwerner can begin conducting interviews and accessing records in the case.

The Newport News Public Schools said in a Wednesday statement that it cannot comment on legal actions but has "worked cooperatively" with authorities and "remains committed to ensuring the well-being and care of all students and staff."

Zwerner resigned from the school after filing the lawsuit. She told NBC News in March that she must continue to undergo physical therapy and struggles with the emotional trauma of that day.

Diane Toscano, a lawyer for Zwerner, said in a statement Wednesday that she remains "surrounded by the support of people who love and care for her, and we are thankful every day that she survived the shooting.

https://www.nbcnews.com/news/us-news/new-details-emerge-6-year-old-boy-shot-virginia-teacher-got-moms-gun-rcna98995

Very sad on so many levels. And you're probably thinking, as a Christian parent, it could never happen to you and your children. Good thoughts -- but what are you doing to ensure a tragedy like this doesn't happen in your family? The life you live in front of your children is what they see and practice. If you're preparing for church and using foul language towards your children to ensure they're ready because you cannot afford to be late, they will likely mimic the same behavior. If you talk violence, disrespect, hatred, bigotry, racism, and other negativities around your children, they'll think it's okay because you're the authority in the house. <u>The parent is the representative of God in the home.</u>

If you attend church on Sundays and at the club on Saturdays, then children live what they learn. If you're a single parent and dating someone and practicing premarital sex, then children see that, and they'll think it's okay. If, as a parent, you cheat on your taxes, shoplift, drink liquor, smoke, watch X-rated movies, or you're easy to instigate a physical fight anywhere, or you're out of order in a parent/teacher's meeting ~ what message does that send to your children? So, as parents who profess Jesus Christ as Lord and Savior, we need to return to Godly consecration, which is being yielded to the Holy Spirit, having a consistent prayer life, studying God's word, and living a lifestyle that glorifies God in every way whether others see it or not.

This era we're living in is different from the past. If you think it's because of the recent global lockdown and the world re-opening, I'm sure your thinking is off. A spirit from hell has been unleashed to destroy our children ~ our Godly seed. That spirit has an evil and aggressive agenda to remove God and His word from the nations. That spirit intends to seduce anyone whose eyes are blinded and cannot discern what's happening. The intent is to steal, kill, and destroy every child and end God's plan and purposes for future generations. That spirit is to capture and mesmerize the young ones into captivity with no return. Why? Because anything God does in the earth, He does it through a man. And the wicked agenda from hell is no new thing. It's the same old, evil scheme that the enemy's executed on the earth ~ from ancient times (see Matthew 2:16-18). Oh, but there's an outcry to all born-again believers in Christ to rise in holiness and righteousness and defend God's purposes. Will you be like Lois and Eunice (Timothy's grandmother and mother) who lived lives that believed and practiced God's word? (2 Timothy 1:5). That same Timothy was mentored by the Apostle Paul who also need-ed a trustworthy person to carry on after he died. Paul chose the zealous, young disciple Timothy.

We'll spend a ton of money on designer clothing, smart devic-es, birthday parties, and vacations and neglect Godly upbringing. We'll even get the most excellent cars and move into family-friendly neighborhoods with beautiful homes for our children. And that's good. I believe in upward mobility. However, those items in and of themselves without God as the center – are empty and void. Smart devices are replacing social interaction, especially in the home, not to mention everywhere else. At-home worship is at an all-time low. Only God knows what happens at the dinner table (if families allow smart devices). We can't afford to put our children at risk of being out of touch with us as parents, especially God. While the world is changing and insisting that we accept questionable, "head-scratching" lifestyles – we must reinforce God's truth at home first and constantly. And note this: if there's a failure, tragedy, calamity, or crisis with your child, the first point of contact is the parent. The school will still call and report to you as the parent that the child is having problems. If your child is arrested, the police will still knock on your door and bring it to your attention. Even worse, the news media will be at your door trying to understand what happened with your child. So, let's pull up our sleeves and do the work. After all, this is our seed. We're responsible for shaping our children to be a generational blessing here, now, and for the future. Last thought: think about the awful harvest of calamity and tragedy we'll reap. Think about how we'll have to give an account for not raising our children in the fear and admonition of the Lord. Consider what it can be like to follow God's plan to raise Godly seed. So, if you're on the Lord's side, let's diligently raise our children God's way!

FOUNDATIONAL SCRIPTURES, PRAYERS AND DECLARATIONS:

> **Isaiah 8:18**
> **Here am I and the children whom the Lord has given me! We are for signs and wonders in Israel from the Lord of hosts Who dwells in Zion. (NKJV)**

Father, in awe of Your wisdom and grace, we stand before You as parents entrusted with the precious gift of children. As Your Word declares, "Here am I and the children whom the Lord has given me! We are for signs and wonders in Israel from the Lord of hosts Who dwells in Zion." (Isaiah 8:18, NKJV). We humbly acknowledge that our children are a blessing and vessels for Your divine purpose.

Lord, we confess that we are grateful for the privilege of nurturing and guiding these young hearts under Your watchful eye. We believe each child is fearfully and wonderfully made, destined to reflect Your glory through signs and wonders in their lives.

Today, we declare our commitment to raising our children in accordance with Your will. We understand that our role extends beyond earthly boundaries; we are called to instill faith, truth, and love into their lives. Just as You dwell in Zion, You reside within our family's foundation, guiding us in wisdom and truth.

We confess that as parents, we are vessels of Your grace, entrusted with the sacred duty of nurturing these young souls. We declare that we will lead by example, teaching them to honor You, to love one another, and to walk in the paths of righteousness.

Lord, we recognize that our children are our legacy and ambassadors of Your kingdom. We confess they are for signs and wonders in our world—manifestations of Your love, grace, and power. We release them into Your capable hands, believing that Your miraculous presence will mark their lives.

In faith and humility, we dedicate our children to You anew. We declare that you order their paths, and their steps are guided by Your unfailing love. We trust in Your promises and embrace the privilege of nurturing them in the light of Your Word.

Thank you, Lord, for this blessed responsibility. May our family be a testament to Your goodness, grace, and glory. In Jesus' name, we pray. Amen.

> **Isaiah 54:13**
> **And all your [spiritual] children shall be disciples**
> **[taught by the Lord and obedient to His will], and**
> **great shall be the peace and undisturbed composure of**
> **your children. (AMPC)**

Father, with hearts full of faith and love, we come before You as parents entrusted with the nurturing of our precious children. Your Word assures us in **Isaiah 54:13, "All your children shall be taught by the Lord, and great shall be the peace of your children." (NKJV)** We embrace this promise and declare it over our family today.

Lord, we confess that our children are not just ours but are also Yours. We believe in Your divine plan for their lives and acknowledge that You are their ultimate Teacher. We trust that as we strive to guide them, You guide them even more profoundly.

We declare that You are intricately involved in every aspect of our children's lives. You teach them through the beauty of creation, the wisdom of Your Word, and the whispers of Your Spirit. Your lessons are woven into their experiences, molding them into individuals who seek truth, love, and compassion.

We confess that Your divine instruction brings them peace that surpasses understanding. Just as You calmed the stormy seas, Your Word anchors them amid life's challenges. Your wisdom equips them to make choices rooted in righteousness and grace.

Lord, we release any anxieties or worries we may have as parents. We entrust our children's growth and development to You, knowing that Your teachings lead to their flourishing. May their hearts be open to Your guidance, and may they find great peace in their relationship with You.

We embrace the promise of Isaiah 54:13 with gratitude and faith. We declare that our children are taught by the Lord, and their lives reflect the peace from knowing You. We stand in awe of Your goodness and deep love for our family.

In the name of Jesus, our Savior, Teacher, and Prince of Peace, we pray. Amen.

Psalm 119:99
I have more understanding than all my teachers, for Your testimonies are my meditation. (NKJV)

Father, we come before You today with hearts full of gratitude and awe for the incredible journey of faith our children are embarking upon. The words of **Psalm 119:99** echo in our minds and hearts: **"I have more understanding than all my teachers, for Your testimonies are my meditation." (NKJV)**

Lord, we thank You for instilling in our children a hunger for Your Word, a thirst for knowledge beyond the confines of a classroom. We are humbled by the depth of understanding they gain through meditating on Your Word. It is a testimony to the transformative power of Your presence in their lives.

As parents, we lift our children to You in prayer. We ask that You continue nurturing their curiosity, quest for truth, and passion for Your teachings. May Your Word be a lamp to their feet and a light to their path, guiding them in every decision, every pursuit, and every interaction.

Grant our children discernment so they may comprehend the profound wisdom within Your testimonies. Let their understanding be not just academic but spiritual, rooted in a deep relationship with You. May their pursuit of understanding be marked by humility, compassion, and a heart that seeks to honor You in all things.

Lord, as our children grow in knowledge and faith, may their understanding serve as a beacon of light to others, drawing people closer to Your truth and grace. In a world that often lacks wisdom, may our children's lives be a testament to the transformative power of meditating on Your Word.

We entrust our children's journey of understanding to You, knowing that Your guidance is infallible, and Your love is boundless. May Your testimonies continue to be a source of inspiration, growth, and peace in their life. In Jesus' name, we pray. Amen.

Deuteronomy 28:13
And the Lord will make you head and not the tail; you
shall be above only, and not be beneath... (NKJV)

With hearts full of hope and trust, we lift our beloved children to You, guided by the promise of Deuteronomy 28:13: "And the Lord will make you the head and not the tail; you shall be above only, and not be beneath..." (NKJV).

Lord, we thank You for the gift of our children's lives, for their unique talents, strengths, and potential. We stand in faith, believing in Your promise to exalt and elevate them. We ask for Your divine guidance and blessings as they navigate the paths of life.

We pray that You continue leading our children on a growth, learning, and achievement journey. May they always walk in the knowledge that You are their constant companion, their Provider, and their strength. As they seek to excel in their endeavors, remind them that they are designed to be leaders, not followers, to be at the forefront of positive change.

Lord, we ask for wisdom for our children so they may make choices aligned with Your will. Help them rise above challenges and difficulties, knowing they are destined for greatness through Your grace. May they inspire others by their actions, integrity, and resilience.

We pray that our children's lives are marked by humility and gratitude, acknowledging that all accomplishments are made possible by Your grace and mercy. May their success be a testament to Your faithfulness and their commitment to living a life that honors You.

Guide our children, dear Lord, and remind them that their value isn't defined by worldly standards but by Your boundless love. Let them find their identity in You, and may they use their position and influence to uplift others, reflecting Your light in all they do.

As parents, we surrender our children into Your care, trusting in Your divine plan for their lives. May they continually experience Your love, protection, and guidance as they embrace the promise of being the head and not the tail. In Jesus' name, we pray. Amen.

Psalms 121:7-8
The Lord shall preserve you from all evil; He shall preserve your soul. The Lord shall preserve your going out and your coming in from this time forth, and even forevermore. (NKJV)

Father, we lift our precious children before You, guided by the assurance of Psalms 121:7-8.

Lord, we are deeply grateful for the gift of our children—beacons of light and hope in our lives. We place them into Your loving hands, trusting in Your promise of protection, guidance, and eternal care.

We decree and declare that You will surround our children with Your divine shield, guarding them against the snares of the world. You will preserve them from all forms of evil, both seen and unseen. You will strengthen their hearts and minds so that they will discern right from wrong and choose paths that lead to righteousness.

Lord, we ask for Your preservation of their souls. Keep their spirits pure and their hearts steadfast in their faith. We decree and declare that they will seek Your presence in all they do, finding comfort, guidance, and solace in the depths of their relationship with You.

We pray for Your watchful care over their daily activities. As they venture out into the world and return to the safety of our home, shield them from harm and lead them along paths of purpose and fulfillment. Preserve their minds, bodies, and spirits, and grant them discernment to navigate life's challenges with Your wisdom.

In moments of uncertainty, remind them of Your unfailing love and unwavering protection. May they find strength in knowing that You are their refuge, their ever-present help in times of need.

Lord, we entrust our children's lives into Your hands, for You are their ultimate Guide and Guardian. Let them experience Your loving care, and may their lives testify to Your faithfulness.

In the name of Jesus, our Savior, we pray. Amen.

Matthew 5:6
**Blessed are those who hunger and thirst for
righteousness, for they shall be filled.**

Father, we thank You for the precious souls You have entrusted to our care. We pray that as we impart Your Word to our children daily, a hunger and thirst for righteousness will burn brightly within them, leading them to seek Your truth, ways, and perfect will in all things.

As parents, we yearn for our children to experience the fullness of Your blessings. May their longing for righteousness draw them closer to You, fostering a deep and abiding relationship with You, the Almighty God. Help them to recognize that the world's offerings are temporary, but the fulfillment of seeking You is everlasting.

We ask that You instill a passion for justice, kindness, and compassion in our children. May their desire for righteousness inspire them to stand up for what is right, to champion the cause of the oppressed, and to extend love and grace to those in need.

Lord, as they journey through life, may their pursuit of righteousness be a guiding light, illuminating their path and shaping their decisions. Strengthen their resolve to make choices that honor You, even when faced with challenges or temptations.

We pray that they will experience the blessedness that comes from seeking You with all their hearts. Fill them with Your wisdom, grace, and understanding, satisfying the hunger of their souls and quenching the thirst of their spirit man.

May our children's lives reflect the righteousness they seek, becoming a living testimony to Your transformative power. As they hunger and thirst for Your righteousness, let them discover the abundant blessings that flow from a life dedicated to You. In Jesus' name, we pray. Amen.

> **Jeremiah 29:11**
> **For I know the thoughts that I think toward you, says the LORD, thoughts of peace and not of evil, to give you a future and a hope.**

I decree and declare that my children are a precious gift entrusted to me by the Lord, and as their parent, I stand and declare the promise of Jeremiah 29:11: "For I know the thoughts that I think toward you, says the LORD, thoughts of peace and not of evil, to give you a future and a hope."

I declare this truth over my children with unwavering faith.

I declare my children are not a product of chance; they are intentionally designed by the loving Creator of the Universe.

I declare that God's thoughts toward my children are peace, love, purpose, and hope. His plans for my children's lives are intricate, beautiful, and full of promise.

I declare that as my children walk through life's journey, they will always find comfort in knowing that God's intentions for them are good. My children are not alone in this path; the Lord's presence goes before them, guiding their steps and illuminating their way.

I declare that even in moments of uncertainty, my children can trust in God's sovereign plan. Their future is secure in His hands, and He has laid out a path that leads to a hopeful destination.

My children have a purpose that transcends the challenges and trials they may encounter, a purpose that contributes to the more remarkable story God is weaving.

I declare that my children are vessels of hope and carriers of His light and glory. As they embrace God's thoughts of peace and goodness, they have nothing missing, nothing broken, and nothing lacking in their lives. My children radiate God's love to those around them. Their actions, choices, and character will reflect God's grace and truth.

I declare that my dear children live with confidence, knowing that their lives are marked by God's unending love. I declare that they are equipped to face each day with courage, wisdom, and a heart full of hope. My children's future is bright because they are held in the palm of God's hand.

I declare that my children always walk in the assurance of Jeremiah 29:11, carrying the promise of a future filled with hope and guided by God's unwavering, never-failing love. In the name of Jesus, amen.

John 10:4
And when he brings out his own sheep, he goes before them; and the sheep follow him, for they know his voice.

Today, I decree and declare that I stand firm in the truth of John 10:4, which proclaims, "And when he brings out his own sheep, he goes before them; and the sheep follow him, for they know his voice."

I declare over my beloved children that they are attuned to the voice of the Good Shepherd. Just as His sheep follow Him because they recognize His voice, so too my children are His sheep, and they recognize and heed the gentle whispers of their Heavenly Father.

I declare that my children's hearts are tuned to God's voice, distinguishing it from the noise of the world. Their spirits are finely attuned to His presence, and they know His voice as one of love, truth, and wisdom.

I declare that my children's ears are closed to the voice of the stranger, to the deceptive whispers that would lead them astray. They discern between the voice of the enemy and the voice of their Savior, and they choose to listen only to the voice that speaks life and purpose into their hearts.

I declare that my children's obedience flows naturally from their recognition of God's voice. They are quick to respond to His guidance and instruction, for they trust in His perfect plan for their lives. Their steps are ordered by the Shepherd's voice, and they walk confidently along the path He lays before them.

I declare that my children's lives are a testimony to their intimate relationship with their Good Shepherd. Just as sheep follow their shepherd, my children follow the call of their Savior with unwavering faith. They are led by His wisdom, protected by His love, and guided by His voice.

In all circumstances, I am confident that my children will follow the voice of their Heavenly Father. They will thrive in His presence, finding peace and purpose in every step they take. I declare that their lives reflect the truth of John 10:4, for they are known and cherished by the Good Shepherd.

Today, I stand firm on the promise of **Psalm 145:4: "One generation shall praise Your works to another, and shall declare Your mighty acts."**

I decree and declare over my precious children that the legacy of God's goodness shall flow seamlessly from one generation to another. Just as those who have gone before have praised His works, I declare that my children will witness and declare His mighty acts in their own lives.

I decree and declare that my life is a testament to God's faithfulness, and this legacy of faith extends to my children. The same presence of God that has guided, protected, and blessed me is now resting upon my children's lives. They inherit the promise of His love, grace, and provision.

I decree and declare that a generational anointing is being imparted to my children. The anointing that has accompanied my journey with God is now flowing down to them. They are marked by His Spirit, equipped for their own unique purposes, and empowered to walk in His ways.

I decree and declare that the God who has done great works in my life is doing the same for my children. As they seek Him and trust in His unfailing love, they will witness His miraculous interventions, experience His healing touch, and encounter His divine guidance.

I decree and declare that my children will carry forward the testimony of God's goodness. Their lives will be a narrative of His faithfulness, and they will confidently declare His mighty acts to the generations that follow. Their testimony will ignite faith, inspire hope, and lead others into a deeper relationship with our Heavenly Father.

In every step of their journey, my children sense the presence of God as a tangible force, leading them, guiding them, and surrounding them with His unwavering love. In the name of Jesus, amen.

A Child of God I Am, Amen! has been written so anyone can read and follow it through successfully. Each chapter was carefully designed and prepared as inspired by the Holy Spirit. We start with a topic or a declaration. From there, the declaration is backed by foundational scriptures followed by confessions. The scriptures chosen aren't all-inclusive. It's just a foundation where you can build upon, 'here a little and there a little' (Isaiah 28:10). At the end of the topic, have your child declare, "A Child of God I Am, Amen!" I added the word amen so that the previous declarations are solidified in the child's heart. When you say **'amen'**...it means the order is firm and fixed; it expresses solemn ratification or agreement; it is binding. Finally, to finish off the topic, end it in prayer. As the parent, take the opportunity to lead your child in prayer based on that chapter. Get your anointing oil and anoint your children often ~ leave no stone unturned. **When you anoint your children, it signifies that they have been set aside and dedicated to the purposes and plans of God**. Applying the anointing oil on your children also signifies the favor and protection of God. (If you don't have any anointing oil at home, I encourage you to purchase a bottle of olive oil at your local store and bring it to your pastor to pray over it, or to your next anointing service ~ if held at your church. The anointing oil dedication is solely for the purposes of application during prayer and consecration). Let your house be a place of prayer where your children know that everything can be settled at the altar of prayer at home.

Next and equally important is that you must **apply the blood of Jesus over your children**. The blood of Jesus will never (and can never) lose its power because it's God's divine blood. John 1:14 says, "Jesus is the only begotten of the Father..." The blood of Jesus is powerful enough for any situation, and that includes your children. We apply the blood of Jesus by declaring it, by applying it. Hebrews 12:24 says, "The blood of Jesus speaks better things than the blood of Abel." The blood of Jesus can destroy sickness, it provides protection to your family. (Also, Rev. 12:11)

Declare:

- By faith in the blood of Jesus, I apply it to my children's lives for divine protection from every evil plan of the enemy.

- Let the blood of Jesus destroy every demonic agenda that's been scheduled for my children. My children will fulfill their God-ordained destinies. They will not be late nor deterred from reaching their God-ordained purposes, in Jesus' name.

- Let the blood of Jesus flush out all inherited sicknesses, evil patterns, and infirmities. Let the blood of Jesus purify their systems. Today, I draw a circle of the blood of Jesus around myself and my children.

Parents, look at your children. They are God's reward to you. While you dress them up in the best you can afford and send them off to school with hopes of preparing them for a great future, you owe it to God, yourself, and your precious children to be the best steward. Many Christian parents leave it to the church to do the grind work. The thing is that your children don't belong to the children's church. They belong to you. Take ownership and raise your Godly seed.

Do you remember the account of Eli (one of the judges in the Old Testament)? While he was judging Israel, eating everything in sight (because he was overweight) – he was a father of two sons, Hophni and Phineas, whom he spared disciplining and checking on their indiscretions. Those two sons of Eli were brazen! They were at the temple, messing with women without any fear of God. The Lord spoke to young Samuel and shared His plans for Eli and his two sons. Very soon, the enemy came and slaughtered Israel. Hophni and Phineas died. Eli died when he heard the news. Phineas' wife went into premature labor and called her son Ichabod, meaning the glory has departed. Reference: 1 Samuel 4.

Apostle Paul's note to his spiritual son, Timothy:

But as for you, continue in what you have learned and have firmly believed, knowing from whom you learned it and how from childhood you have been acquainted with the sacred writings, which are able to make you wise for salvation through faith in Christ Jesus. All Scripture is breathed out by God and profitable for teaching, for reproof, for correction, and for training in righteousness, that the man of God may be complete, equipped for every good work. 2 Timothy 3:14-17 (ESV)

A PRAYER FOR THE PARENTS:

Father, In Jesus' name – I pray for the parents who'll read and frequently use this book. To You, God, be all the glory, honor, and praise. Father, may each parent rise to the call and duty of raising Godly seed to bring you great glory and honor. May each parent be diligent in their walk with You, whether they're being seen or not. If any parent has been going down the wrong road with their children, may they repent and make a complete turnaround to bring you glory and honor. In the name of Jesus, amen.

Now, for your children:

- ✠ May your children rise like mighty, strong, confident, and competent boys and girls (and then men and women) because of the Word you've faithfully planted in their lives. In Jesus name!

- ✠ May the Spirit of the Lord mount garrison around you and your children. In Jesus name!

- ✠ May the arrow by day, the destruction that would lay waste at noonday, and the pestilence that would stalk in the darkness be reversed and sent back to hell – because the Word of God mounts garrisons around your children. In Jesus name!

✠ May the deceptive devices and the craftiness of men to discourage, deceive, confuse, and trap your children -- be dismantled and rubbished by the fire of God! In Jesus name!

✠ May your children know the voice of the Holy Ghost through family prayer time and personal worship time. In Jesus name!

✠ May your children experience the fire and power of the Holy Ghost in your local church and children's services. In Jesus name!

✠ May your children see and experience the mighty power of God's love through miracles, signs, and wonders! In Jesus name!

✠ May your children be raised to be leaders to reign and rule in the marketplace, education, science, government, business, the arts, and any other industry for the glory of God, in Jesus' name. Amen.

✠ May your children be sound in mind and body, with nothing missing or broken. In Jesus name!

✠ May your children be a blessing to their generation. In Jesus name!

✠ May your children bring you joy and not shame or sorrow. In Jesus name!

✠ May your children be in the right place at the right time. In Jesus name!

✠ May your children never be ashamed of the gospel of Jesus Christ. In Jesus name!

✠ May your children experience an authentic and personal relationship with the Lord Jesus Christ and the Holy Spirit. In Jesus name! Amen!

I Decree and Declare:

- ⳨ Your children are the seed of the righteous and are blessed (empowered to prosper in every arena of life). In Jesus name!

- ⳨ Your children, the seed of the righteous, are delivered. The generation of the upright is blessed! In Jesus name!

- ⳨ As parents, by the blood of Jesus and the covenant of mercy, you will never see your children in crisis, calamity, or evil emergencies. In Jesus name!

- ⳨ May the Holy oil of distinction, gladness, and joy always be your portion and the portion of your children now and forever.

In the mighty name of Jesus Christ, AMEN!

GOD'S WORD
IN MY HEART

In the garden of my heart, I hide God's precious words side by side. Like seeds, they grow, solid and deep, guiding me as I laugh and leap.

I hide His words like treasures bright, gems that shine in the darkest night.

They give me courage, strength, and grace, no matter where I run or race.

When storms may come with thunder loud, His words are my shelter, a loving shroud. I hold them close, a secret part; they're etched forever in my heart.

In every joy, in every tear, God's words are whispered, oh so clear.

They light my path; they show the way, helping me through each brand-new day.

So, I'll keep hiding His words within – a precious bond that's never thin.

For in my heart, they'll always stay, guiding me in life's amazing way.

GOD IS REAL

GOD'S WORD:

Before the world began, there was the Word. The Word was with God, and the Word was God. John 1:1, ICB

Ever since the world was created, people have seen the earth and sky. Through everything God made, they can clearly see His invisible qualities—His eternal power and divine nature. So they have no excuse for not knowing God. Romans 1:20, NLT

But for us, There is one God, the Father, by whom all things were created, and for whom we live. And there is one Lord, Jesus Christ, through whom all things were created, and through whom we live. 1 Corinthians 8:6, NLT

God says, Then Jesus told him, "You believe because you have seen me. Blessed are those who believe without seeing me." John 20:29, NLT

Before the mountains were born, and before You created the earth and the world, You are God. You have always been, and You will always be. Psalms 90:2, ICB

No pagan god is like You, O Lord. None can do what You do! All the nations You made will come and bow before you, Lord;

they will praise Your holy name. For You are great and perform wonderful deeds. You alone are God. Psalms 86:8-10, NLT

God said to Moses, "I AM WHO I AM" and He said, "Thus you shall say to the sons of Israel, 'I AM has sent me to you.'" Exodus 3:14

However, there is a God in heaven who reveals mysteries, and He has made known to King Nebuchadnezzar what will take place in the latter days. This was your dream and the visions in your mind while on your bed. Daniel 2:28

All honor and glory to God forever and ever! He is the eternal King, the unseen one who never dies; he alone is God. Amen. 1 Timothy 1:17, NLT

"I am the Alpha and the Omega," says the Lord God, "who is and who was and who is to come, the Almighty." Revelations 1:8

Confession:

God is real.

I serve a living God – even the devil knows that God is real!

The God I serve hears and answers me when I call on Him.

The God I serve honors my faith in Him.

God is the God of my parent(s).

My God is the God of my family.

Although I can't see God, I can see His beautiful creations...and I am one of them.

I can't see the wind, but I can feel it.

I can see the wind when the leaves on the trees go from side to side.

God is like the wind. I can see Him in His Word.

I can see and feel His love and compassion when He healed the sick, opened blind eyes, made the lame walk, raised the dead and fed the multitudes of people when they came to hear Him and be healed.

God is real. There is no other God except the God of the Bible.[1]

God has ears. He hears me when I call His name.

God has eyes. His eyes are always on me. I am the apple of His eye.

I am the center of God's love.

God has hands. He will hold my hand. He will guide me by His hand. He will provide when I am in need.

God has a heart. He is touched when I am happy. He is touched when I am sad. He is touched by my faith in Him.

God never changes. He never gets tired. He never ages. He is eternal. He reigns forever. He is the true and living God.

The other gods cannot hear, speak or touch. They are the gods that someone created. The God I serve was always there. He will always be.

A Child of God I am, amen!

[Note to parent: Lead your child in prayer based on this topic].

---

1   For the LORD is great, and greatly to be praised: He is to be feared above all gods. For all the gods of the nations are idols: But the LORD made the heavens. Psalms 96:4-5 (KJV)

GOD'S WORD IS TRUTH

GOD'S WORD:

"The first thing to know about your word is that it is true." Psalms 119:160, CEB

"Your word, O LORD, will last forever; it is eternal in heaven." Psalm 119:89, GNT

"And now, Sovereign Lord, you are God; You always keep Your promises, and You have made this wonderful promise to me." 2 Samuel 7:28, GNT

"I have hidden Your word in my heart, that I might not sin against You." Psalms 119:11, NLT

"Every word of God proves true; He is a shield to those who take refuge in him." Proverbs 30:5

"The grass withers, the flower fades, but the word of our God will stand forever." Isaiah 40:8

"Heaven and earth will pass away, but My words will not pass away." Matthew 24:35

Confession:

I serve the true and living God.

His Word is true.

His Word is all-powerful.

His Word can be trusted.

His Word is His promise.

God is a promise keeper.

God has kept all His promises, and not one has failed.

People may or may not keep their promises. They may fail or let me down. But God's Word is true. I can read it any time. Memorize it and trust Him with His Word. He will not fail me.

When I read through the Bible stories, every promise God made, He came through without fail.

Some people lie; they speak lies. But God cannot lie. He keeps His Word. His Word is true, forever and ever.

Every day, I will read and memorize God's Word. I will hide it in my heart so that I won't do the wrong thing. I'll do the right thing every day because God's Word is in my heart.

Every day, I will keep hearing and saying God's Word. His Word makes me strong and confident.

Father, You are the source of everlasting truth. You are good and wise and have shown Your wisdom through Your Word.

Father, thank you for Your truth. It is a lamp to my feet, and it lights my path.

Father, help me to treasure Your Words in my heart.

Father, help me live by every Word from Your mouth.

Father, help me store up Your Word in my heart so that I might not sin against You. Help me to follow Your path and obey Your commands.

A Child of God I am, amen!

[Note to parent: Lead your child in prayer based on this topic].

GOD'S WORD IS MY FOUNDATION

GOD'S WORD:

"Therefore, everyone who hears these words of Mine and acts on them, may be compared to a wise man who built his house on the rock." Matthew 7:24

CONFESSION:

I'm building something great. And it starts with God's Word.

God's Word is true.

God's Word can never fail.

God's Word comes first.

God's Word leads me every day.

God's Word keeps me every day.

God's Word guides me every day.

God's Word gives me hope.

God's Word gives me a bright future.

I am a smart child because I start with God's Word daily!

I am a reader and a doer of God's Word.

God's Word is love.

God's Word is life.

God's Word guides me.

A Child of God I am, amen!

[Note to parent: Lead your child in prayer based on this topic].

I AM CREATED IN THE IMAGE OF GOD

GOD'S WORD:

"Oh yes, You shaped me first inside, then out; You formed me in my mother's womb. I thank You, High God—you're breathtaking! Body and soul, I am marvelously made! I worship in adoration—what a creation! You know me inside and out, You know every bone in my body; You know exactly how I was made, bit by bit, how I was sculpted from nothing into something. Like an open book, You watched me grow from conception to birth; all the stages of my life were spread out before You, the days of my life all prepared before I'd even lived one day."

Psalms 139, The Message Bible

"So, God created human beings in His image. In the image of God, He created them. He created them male and female." Genesis 1:27 International Children's Bible

"Every good and perfect gift comes from above, coming down from the Father of lights."

James 1:17, NIV

"The Lord your God is with you, the Mighty Warrior who saves. He will take great delight in you; he will rejoice over you with singing." Zephaniah 3:17, NIV

"For we are God's masterpiece. He has created us anew in Christ Jesus, so we can do the good things he planned for us long ago." Ephesians 2:10 NLT

"I can do all things through Christ who strengthens me." Philippians 4:13 KJV

CONFESSION:

God formed me in my mother's womb.

I am God's marvelous creation.

I have the perfect skin color.

I have the perfect eye color.

I have the perfect hair texture.

I have a unique fingerprint.

I am distinct from everyone else, so there is no room for comparison.

No matter how old I get, I will always be a child of God. I am my Father's child and loved by Him with no strings attached. I don't have to work for God's love.

God loves me, God loves me, and I will keep saying it over and over. God's love for me has no limits, no boundaries. Amen!

Confession for Boys:

I am a handsome **[BOY]** inside and out because that's the way God created me. God makes no mistakes. I came into the world at the right time, and He's got a great plan for me.

Confession for Girls:

I am a beautiful **[GIRL]** inside and out because that's the way God created me. God makes no mistakes. I came into the world at the right time, and He's got a great plan for me.

Children continue the Confession:

God, my Father, knew me and watched me grow from the time I was conceived until it was time to be birthed into this world.

God makes no mistakes. So, I am a perfect gift from God.

God is always with me. He gets so excited over me; He rejoices and sings over me.

I am God's masterpiece.

It was planned a long time ago for me to do great things for God.

I'm a world changer. I was born for greatness because that's what God said about me.

I am a beautiful child.

God delights in me.

I am super intelligent.

I am gifted.

I am talented.

Because God created me with His love, I am very confident. No one can tell me otherwise.

My skin color, hair texture, and eye color – are all a part of God's plan. I am a good-looking kid!

No one can tell me otherwise. I love being me because no one in the world is quite like me!

I have the potential to do anything that God wants me to do.

God lives in me, and He's very big. God's very large. God is very great. And because God is BIG, LARGE, and GREAT...I am too!

I can do all things through Christ Jesus that gives me strength.

I was created in God's very image. GOD IS GREAT, AND SO AM I!

There's greatness on the inside of me. No one can take it away.

I was born to be great and to be a huge blessing. I was born to stand out and make a difference in my generation.

I am God's AMAZING workmanship, created to do AMAZING THINGS![2]

I was born for greatness, so watch out, world!

A Child of God I am, amen!

[Note to parent: Lead your child in prayer based on this topic].

---

2   Ephesians 2:10

YOU'RE GOD'S CHILD – THAT'S WHO YOU ARE

In fields of love where children play, God's Word shines bright, a guiding ray.

It tells the truth of who you are: a cherished child and a shining star.

You're fearfully and wonderfully made, in God's own image, beautifully laid.

With care, He formed your precious frame; in Christ, you bear a cherished name.

You are a light that brightly gleams, a part of God's incredible dreams.

His love in you will always stay, guiding you along life's way.

No matter where your path may lead, in Christ, you have all that you need.

A heart so full of grace and love, a child of God, watched from above.

So, stand tall, little one, don't fear, for in Christ's love, you're always near.

You're unique, precious, and so dear, in God's embrace, forever clear.

Remember who you are each day, a child of God, come what may.

With love and grace, you're always blessed; in Christ, you find eternal rest.

I AM DIVINELY PROTECTED

GOD'S WORD:

Psalm 91, NLT

¹ Those who live in the shelter of the Most High will find rest in the shadow of the Almighty.

² This I declare about the Lord: He alone is my refuge, my place of safety; He is my God, and I trust him.

³ For He will rescue me from every trap and protect me from deadly disease.

⁴ He will cover me with His feathers. He will shelter me with His wings. His faithful promises are my armor and protection.

⁵ I will not be afraid of the terrors of the night, nor the arrow that flies in the day.

⁶ I will not dread the disease that stalks in darkness, nor the disaster that strikes at midday.

⁷ Though a thousand fall at my side, though ten thousand are dying around me these evils will not touch me.

⁸ I just open your eyes and see how the wicked are punished.

⁹ If I make the Lord my refuge, if I make the Most High my shelter,

¹⁰ no evil will conquer me; no plague will come near my home.

¹¹ For God will order His angels to protect me wherever I go.

¹² The angels will hold me up with their hands so I won't even hurt my foot on a stone.

¹³ I will trample upon lions and cobras; I will crush fierce lions and serpents under my feet!

¹⁴ The Lord says, "He will rescue those who love Him. He will protect those who trust in His name.

¹⁵ When I call on Him, He will answer; He will be with me in trouble. He will rescue and honor me.

¹⁶ He will reward me with a long life and give me His salvation."

Psalms 91, ICB

¹ Those who go to God Most High for safety will be protected by God All-Powerful.

² I will say to the Lord, "You are my place of safety and protection. You are my God, and I trust you."

³ God will save me from hidden traps and from deadly diseases.

⁴ He will protect me like a bird spreading its wings over its young. His truth will be like my armor and shield.

⁵ I will not fear any danger by night or an arrow during the day.

⁶ I will not be afraid of diseases that come in the dark or sickness that strikes at noon.

⁷ At my side 1,000 people may die, or even 10,000 right beside me. But I will not be hurt.

⁸ I will only watch what happens. I will see the wicked punished.

⁹ The Lord is my protection. I have made God Most High my place of safety.

¹⁰ Nothing bad will happen to me. No disaster will come to my home.

[11] He has put his angels in charge of me. They will watch over me wherever I go.

[12] They will catch me with their hands. And I will not hit my foot on a rock.

[13] I will walk on lions and cobras. I will step on strong lions and snakes.

[14] The Lord says, "If someone loves me, I will save him. I will protect those who know me.

[15] They will call to me, and I will answer them. I will be with them in trouble. I will rescue them and honor them.

[16] I will give them a long, full life. They will see how I can save."

CONFESSION:

I am God's child.

I stay in prayer, and He keeps me safe under His shadow.

God promised to protect me from every trap.

He promised to keep me from deadly sickness.

He covers me like a hen that covers her baby chicks.

God's promises are faithful, and they are my protection. I feel safe because of His promises.

Although viruses and diseases are everywhere, God is my protection. I am A-okay under God's wings.

If ever I am in a danger zone, God will send His angels to guard and protect me from all harm.

God will punish the wicked.

When I call out God's name, God will answer me.

God promised never to leave me alone. So I don't have to be afraid.

He will come and get me out of it if I am in a danger zone.

I am divinely protected from terrorism, bullying, teasing, or any physical or emotional harm. My Angels are with me all day and all night. They shield and protect me.

If anyone ever tries to harm me or if I am in a dangerous zone, the Angels of God will cover and protect me and get me out of every harmful situation every single time.

God will give me a long, strong, and beautiful life.

No matter how tough things get, or how crazy it may seem around me -- one thing I am sure of, God will never leave me.

God is with me everywhere I go! He will never leave me.

God has not given me fear; fear is of the devil! God gives perfect gifts. God has given me power, love and a sound mind.[3]

At home, God is with me.

At school, God is with me.

At afterschool activities, God is with me.

On the bus, God is with me.

On the playground, God is with me.

On field trips, God is with me.

At church, God is with me.

Wherever I am...

Wherever I go...

God is with me ~ all the time.

I am born of God so the evil one can't touch me.[4]

Nothing can separate or cut me off from God's love.[5]

> **"I am dwelling in the secret place of the Most High God. I am abiding under the shadow of the Almighty. I am saying of the Lord, He is my refuge, my fortress,**

---

3   1 Timothy 1:7
4   1 John 5:18
5   Romans 8:35-39

> **My God -- in Him will I trust. Amen." (Psalms 91, paraphrased for confession)**

A Child of God I am, amen!

[Note to parent: Lead your child in prayer based on this topic].

GOD LOVES ME

GOD'S WORD:

God says, "I've never quit loving you and never will. Expect love, love and more love!"

Jeremiah 31:3 – The Message Bible

Certainly, the faithful love of the Lord hasn't ended; certainly, God's compassion isn't through! They are renewed every morning. Great is Your faithfulness. Lamentations 3:22-23, CEB

Your love is better than life. I will praise you. Psalms 63:3, ICB

The mountains may shift, and the hills may be shaken, but My faithful love won't shift from you, and My covenant of peace won't be shaken, says the LORD, the One who pities you. Isaiah 54:10, CEB

But you, my Lord, are a God of compassion and mercy; You are very patient and full of faithful love. Psalms 86:15, CEB

The Lord your God is in your midst—a warrior bringing victory. He will create calm with His love; He will rejoice over you with singing. Zephaniah 3:17, CEB

Know now then that the Lord your God is the only true God! He is the faithful God, who keeps the covenant and proves loyal to everyone who loves him and keeps his commands—even to the thousandth generation! Deuteronomy 7:9, CEB

Know now then that the Lord your God is the only true God! He is the faithful God, who keeps the covenant and proves loyal to everyone who loves Him and keeps His commands—even to the thousandth generation! 1 Chronicles 16:34, CEB

Your faithful love is priceless, God! Humanity finds refuge in the shadow of your wings. Psalms 36:7, CEB

But you, Lord, my Lord! — act on my behalf for the sake of Your name; deliver me because Your faithful love is so good. Psalm 109:21, CEB

This is how the love of God is revealed to us: God has sent his only Son into the world so that we can live through him. This is love: it is not that we loved God but that He loved us and sent His Son as the sacrifice that deals with our sins. 1 John 4:9-10, CEB

Confession:

God loves me. Always did, always will!

God's heart for me is full of love, and I can depend on Him to love me just as much every day!

No matter how the world changes around me, He is always guiding me.

I will make mistakes, but God loves me unconditionally; God will give me grace and forgiveness.

God's love for me will never change.

God's love for me is ever constant.

God's love causes me to be strong and not afraid.

God knows my name. He knows me from the inside out.

I belong to God, and He belongs to me.

God loves me with no strings attached.

God loved me first before I was even born, and the proof is the life of my savior Jesus Christ, who came to free me from sin.

I don't need to try to earn God's love. God's love for me is automatic and will never stop.

God's love provides safety and comfort.

God's thoughts towards me are super special.

God's love makes me secure because He loves me.

God's love will never fail or run out. Never ever!

A Child of God I am, amen!

[Note to parent: Lead your child in prayer based on this topic].

GOD IS MY PROVIDER; HE KEEPS HIS PROMISES

GOD'S WORD (taken from the *International Children's Bible translation – ICB*):

God is my Provider	God keeps His promises
Phil 4:19: My God will use His wonderful riches in Christ Jesus to give you everything you need.	**Joshua 21:45**: He kept every promise he had made to the Israelites. No promises failed. Each one came true.
Acts 14:17: Yet He did things to prove He is real: He shows kindness to you. He gives you rain from heaven and crops at the right times. He gives you food and fills your hearts with joy.	**Luke 1:38**: Mary said, "I am the servant girl of the Lord. Let this happen to me as you say!" Then the angel went away.

Psalms 146:7-9: The Lord does what is fair for those who have been wronged, He gives food to the hungry. The Lord sets the prisoners free. The Lord gives sight to the blind. The Lord lifts up people who are in trouble. The Lord loves those who do it right. The Lord protects the foreigners. He defends the orphans and widows. But He overthrows the wicked.	**Philippians 1:6**: God began doing a good work in you. And He will continue it until it is finished when Jesus Christ comes again. I am sure of that.
1 Samuel 2:8: The Lord raises the poor from the dust. And He picks needy people up from the ashes. He lets the poor sit with princes. He lets them sit on a throne of honor. The foundations of the earth belong to the Lord. The Lord set the world upon them.	**Galatians 6:9**: We must not become tired of doing good. We will receive our harvest of eternal life at the right time. We must not give up!
Deuteronomy 2:7: The Lord your God has blessed everything you have done. He has protected you while you traveled through this large desert. The Lord your God has been with you these 40 years. You have had everything you needed.	**1 Kings 8:56**: "Praise the Lord! He promised He would give rest to His people Israel. And He has given us rest! The Lord has kept all the good promises He gave through His servant Moses.
1 Chronicles 29:12: Riches and honor come from You. You rule everything. You have power and strength to make anyone great and strong.	**2 Corinthians 1:20**: Where is the wise person? Where is the educated person? Where is the philosopher of our times? God has made the wisdom of the world foolish.

GOD'S WORD (taken from the *International Children's Bible translation – ICB*):

God is my Provider	God keeps His promises
Psalm 68:9: God, you sent much rain. You refreshed your tired land.	**Romans 4:21**: Abraham felt sure that God was able to do the thing that God promised.
Matthew 6:26: Look at the birds in the air. They don't plant or harvest or store food in barns. But your heavenly Father feeds the birds. And you know that you are worth much more than the birds.	**Hebrews 10:23**: Let us hold firmly to the hope that we have confessed. We can trust God to do what He promised.
2 Peter 1:3: Jesus has the power of God. His power has given us everything we need to live and to serve God. We have these things because we know him. Jesus called us by his glory and goodness.	**Hebrews 10:36**: You must hold on, so you can do what God wants and receive what He has promised.
Matthew 6:31-33: Don't worry and say, 'What will we eat?' or 'What will we drink?' or 'What will we wear?' All the people who don't know God keep trying to get these things. And your Father in heaven knows that you need them. The thing you should want most is God's kingdom and doing what God wants. Then all these things you need will be given to you.	**Numbers 23:19**: God is not a man. He will not lie. God is not a human being. He does not change His mind. What He says He will do, He does. What He promises, He keeps.

Confession:

My God, the faithful God, provides for all my needs, including my family and friends. When I pray for my friends and strangers, God will supply their needs.

My God is very kind.

He sends rain when the earth and ground are dry.

He provides food for the hungry.

He helps needy people.

He lifts those that are low and hurting.

He sets the captives free.

God works through me and those who love Him to help other people.

He gives me everything I need.

I don't have to worry about what to eat or what I'm going to wear. God already knows I need those things.

All I need to do is make Him first by saying thank you as soon as I wake up in the morning.

All I need to do is give Him praise and read His Word.

All I need to do is love Him and be a light to my family and friends. Then, God will provide everything I need.

The God I serve keeps His promises. He is not like people who lie and tell untruths.

My God never changes His mind. What He says, He will do. He keeps His promises.

I will keep holding on to God's promises and receive what He promised me.

I am like Father Abraham, who kept believing in God because he called God faithful.

Every promise God made to the children of Israel, God kept His promise.

God never changes. He will do as He said.

His Word never goes back to Him unmet.

My God is faithful.

A Child of God I am, amen!

[Note to parent: Lead your child in prayer based on this topic].

HONOR; HELPING OTHERS

GOD'S WORD:

Honor	Helping Others
Ephesians 6:1-3: Children, obey your parents the way the Lord wants. This is the right thing to do. The command says, "Honor your father and mother." This is the first command that has a promise with it. The promise is: "Then everything will be well with you, and you will have long life on the earth." (International Children's Bible translation)	**Galatians 6:2**: Help carry one another's burdens, and in this way you will obey the law of Christ. (Good News Translation)
Romans 13:1: All of you must obey the government rulers. No one rules unless God has given him the power to rule. And no one rules without that power from God. (International Children's Bible translation)	**Hebrews 13:16**: Do not forget to do good and to help one another, because these are the sacrifices that please God. (Good News Translation)

Romans 13:7: Pay, then, what you owe them; pay them our personal and property taxes, and show respect and honor for them all. (Good News Translation)	**John 15:12**: My commandment is this: love one another, just as I love you. (Good News Translation)
1 Timothy 1:17: To the eternal King, immortal and invisible, the only God ~ to Him be honor and glory forever and ever! (Good News Translation)	**Proverbs 19:17**: When you give to the poor, it is like lending to the Lord, and the Lord will pay you back. (Good News Translation)
1 Timothy 5:17: The elders who do good work as leaders should be considered worthy of receiving double pay, especially those who work hard at preaching and teaching. (Good News Translation)	**Romans 12:13**: Share your belongings with your needy fellow Christians and open your home to strangers. (Good News Translation)
1 Peter 2:17: Show respect for all people. Love the brothers and sisters of God's family. Respect God. Honor the king. (International Children's Bible translation)	**Proverbs 3:27**: Whenever you possibly can, do good to those who need it. (Good News Translation)

Confession:

I honor and respect my mother and father. I honor and respect my grandparents. I honor and respect my aunts and uncles. I honor and respect my teachers. I honor and respect all adults.

I speak to them with respect.

I respond to them in love.

I always have a good attitude towards them.

God sent my parents to protect, teach, and raise me.

I am never rude or disrespectful.

I never respond rudely or disrespectfully.

When I honor my parents and elders, it will go well with me always!

I honor the rules of the road. When the red light is on, I know it means to stop.

When the crossing guard says 'go,' I will proceed and go. When they say, 'stop,' I will stop.

I will honor my pastor and teachers in the Lord. They are God's servants. They work hard to study God's word. They pray before God to bring me the Word of God every time we meet. They are worthy of double honor.

I show respect for all people, no matter what color they are.

I will love my brothers and sisters in Christ. They are the family of God.

I am learning right now to pay my dues on time. I will not be late.

When I honor God, God honors me.

The God I serve is worthy of honor, love, and reverence. I will always be loving and grateful to Him.

I will do my best to help those who need help.

God is pleased when I help others who are in need.

I love others just like God loves me.

Whenever possible, I'll do good to others because it pleases God.

A Child of God I am, amen!

[Note to parent: Lead your child in prayer based on this topic].

CHILDREN --
HONOR GOD

In a world that's wide and grand, sometimes, you might need to stand.

Stand alone and strong and true, doing what's right in all you do.

Even if the path seems tough and the road feels a little rough ~

Remember, you're never truly alone; God's with you, His love is shown.

When you make choices that are kind, and in your heart, God's love you find -- You're shining bright, a guiding light, bringing goodness to the darkest night.

So let your life be like a song, a melody that's true and strong ~

Even if you walk a path unknown, let your life honor God alone.

You have the strength deep inside to let God's love be your guide ~

With courage, faith, and love to share, you'll make the world a better place.

So don't be afraid to take a stand and do what's right, hand in hand --

Even if you have to do it on your own, your life can still shine brightly shown.

JESUS SACRIFICED HIS LIFE FOR ME

GOD'S WORD:

John 3:16-17: For God loved the world so much that He gave His only Son, so that everyone who believes in him may not die but have eternal life. For God did not send His Son into the world to be its judge, but to be its savior. (Good News Translation)
Ephesians 5:2: Your life must be controlled by love, just as Christ loved us and gave His life for us as sweet-smelling offering and sacrifices that pleases God. (Good News Translation)

John 14:6: Jesus answered him, "I am the way, the truth, and the life; no one goes to the Father except by me. (Good News Translation)

Matthew 20:28: So it is with the Son of Man. The Son of Man did not come for other people to serve him. He came to serve others. The Son of Man came to give his life to save many people. (International Children's Bible)

Confession:

Adam, the first man, sinned against God.

As a result of Adam's sin, the whole world was born in sin. We needed a savior to pay the price for Adam's sin and bring us back into a relationship with God.

God loved humanity so much. The only way to bring humanity back into fellowship with Him would be to send His son to die for the world.

So, God sent His son (Jesus) as a sacrifice for the sins of the world.

Jesus sacrificed His life for me.

He died for my sins and everyone else's.

He suffered on the cross with the sins of the world. Anyone who believes in Jesus will have eternal life.

The only way to God is through Jesus Christ.

Jesus Christ is the savior of the world.

Jesus came to serve others. He came to save all people from their sins.

I repent and confess my sins. I make [made] a decision to follow Jesus Christ as my Lord.

I am saved from my sins.

A Child of God I am, amen!

[Note to parent: Lead your child in prayer based on this topic].

IF I SIN, GOD WILL FORGIVE ME WHEN I REPENT

I FORGIVE OTHERS AS CHRIST HAS FORGIVEN ME

GOD'S WORD:

God's word says, "But if we confess our sins, he will forgive our sins. We can trust God. He does what is right. He will make us clean from all the wrongs we have done." 1 John 1:9 ICB

Acts 3:19, "Repent therefore and turn back that your sins may be blotted out." ESV

Psalms 103:2, "As far as the east is from the west, so far [has] He removed our transgressions from us." ESV

Ephesians 4:32, "Be kind to one another, tenderhearted, forgiving one another, as God in Christ forgave you." MEV

1 John 2:1-2, "My little children, I am writing these things to you so that you may not sin. But if anyone does sin, we have an advocate with the Father, Jesus Christ, the righteous." MEV

Romans 8:1, "There is therefore now no condemnation for those who are in Christ Jesus." MEV

Matthew 18:21-22, "Then Peter came to Jesus and asked, "Lord, when my brother sins against me, how many times must I forgive him? Should I forgive him as many as 7 times?" Jesus answered, "I tell you, you must forgive him more than 7 times. You must forgive him even if he does wrong to you 70 times 7." ICB

Matthew 6:15, "But if you don't forgive the wrongs of others, then your Father in heaven will not forgive the wrong things you do." ICB

Confession:

Father, in Jesus name, Your Word says, "My dear children, I write this letter to you so that you will not sin. But if anyone does sin, we have Jesus Christ to help us. He is the Righteous One. He defends us before God the Father." 2 John 1 (ICB)

I know that I'll make mistakes and sin because I'm human. But I desire so much to please You, Father.

I am grateful that Your word says that Jesus Christ will help me. He will be right by my side to help me when I come before you and ask for forgiveness.

I am grateful that Your mercies and lovingkindness last forever and never run out. I only desire to love You with my whole heart. I don't have to be afraid. I know that when I sin, I can pray and repent immediately. And, You'll hear me and receive my prayers. Thank you, Jesus. Amen.

When people hurt me or do wrong things against me, I will forgive them ~ just as you forgive me over and over.

A Child of God I am, amen!

[Note to parent: Lead your child in prayer based on this topic].

THANKSGIVING, PRAISE AND WORSHIP

GOD'S WORD:

1 Thessalonians 5:18, "Give thanks whatever happens. That is what God wants for you in Christ Jesus." (ICB)

Psalms 7:17, "I praise the Lord because he does what is right. I sing praises to the name of the Lord Most High." (ICB)

1 John 3:1, "The Father has loved us so much! He loved us so much that we are called children of God. And we really are his children. But the people in the world do not understand that we are God's children, because they have not known him." (ICB)

1 Chronicles 16:34, "Thank the Lord because He is good. His love continues forever." (ICB)

Psalms 9:1-2, "I will praise you, Lord, with all my heart. I will tell all the miracles you have done. I will be happy because of you. God Most High, I will sing praises to Your name." (ICB)

Psalm 100:1-3, "Shout to the Lord, all the earth. Serve the Lord with joy. Come before him with singing. Know that the Lord is God. He made us, and we belong to him." (ICB)

Psalms 34:3, "Oh, magnify the LORD with me, And let us exalt His name together. (NKJV)

Psalms 28:7, "The Lord is my strength and shield. I trust Him, and He helps me. I am very happy. And I praise Him with my song." (ICB)

Psalm 13:6, "I sing to the Lord because he has taken care of me." (ICB)

Confession:

When I wake up in the morning, I'll remember to say, "Thank you, Father God."

When I lay down at night, I'll remember to say, "Thank you, Father God."

Lord, You are good, and your loving-kindness endures forever. Your love towards me continues forever.

The Lord is my strength and my protection. I can always trust Him, and He will always keep me.

My Father, You make me glad. You fill my heart with joy. I will sing praises to Your name all day long.

You're my Strength, Protection, Provider, Helper, Healer, and much more. I will worship You and give You thanks for all You are to me and for everything You have done.

I will praise You, Lord with all my heart for all You've done for me. With all my strength, I will praise You, Lord!

You are great and worthy of praise! You are the true and living God. Men made all the other gods. But You are the Most High God, and there's no one like You!

I'm not going to let any rock take my place to praise You.

I will not be quiet! I will not be silent, for You are too good! I will open my mouth and lift my hands to praise You in singing and telling You how much I love You.

My Father, You have my joyful praise and worship forever and ever!

Hallelujah, Hallelujah...amen!

A Child of God I am, amen!

[Note to parent: Lead your child in prayer based on this topic].

THE PRAISES FROM THE HEART OF A CHILD

In a world so wide, so wild and free –a child's heart beats with joyful glee.

With every giggle and with every smile, we praise God's love, mile after mile.

Through meadows green and skies so blue, in every petal with morning dew ~

A child's voice rises like a song, praising God's gifts all day long.

In whispers of leaves that dance and play, in the warmth of the sun's golden ray --A child's gratitude, pure and bright, fills the world with a radiant light.

With laughter echoing like a gentle stream, in dreams that twinkle like a starry gleam -- a child's heart knows how to impart praise to God, the Creator's art.

From tiny hands to feet that run, in every adventure, under the sun ~

A child's love for life unfurls, praising God, who colors our world.

So let the joy of childhood be a song of praise, forever free.

With every heartbeat, with every start, praise to God from a child's pure heart.

GOD IS MY HEALER

GOD'S WORD:

But the sun of righteousness will rise on those revering my name; healing will be in its wings so that you will go forth and jump about like calves in the stall. Malachi 4:2 (CEB)

The Lord said, "If you are careful to obey the Lord your God, do what God thinks is right, pay attention to his commandments, and keep all of his regulations, then I won't bring on you any of the diseases that I brought on the Egyptians. I am the Lord who heals you." Exodus 15:26 (ICB)

If you worship the Lord your God, the Lord will bless your bread and your water. I'll take sickness away from you. Exodus 23:25 (ICB)

The Lord will take away all disease from you. You will not have the terrible diseases that were in Egypt. But He will give them to your enemies. Deuteronomy 7:15 (ICB)

You must completely obey the Lord your God. And you must carefully follow all His commands I am giving you today. Then the Lord your God will make you greater than any other nation on earth. ² Obey the Lord your God. Then all these blessings will come and stay with you: Deut. 28:1-2 (ICB)

Today I ask heaven and earth to be witnesses. I am offering you life or death, blessings or curses. Now, choose life! Then you and your children may live. Deut. 30:19 (ICB)

He kept every promise he had made to the Israelites. No promises failed. Each one came true. Joshua 21:45 (ICB)

The Lord has kept all the good promises he gave through his servant Moses.

1 Kings 8:56b (CEB)

I will not die, but live. And I will tell what the Lord has done. ~ Psalm 118:17 (ICB)

I will not break my agreement. I will not change what I have said. Psalm 89:34 (ICB)

My child, pay attention to my words. Listen closely to what I say. Don't ever forget my words. Keep them deep within your heart. These words are the secret to life for those who find them. They bring health to the whole body. ~ Proverbs 4:20-22

So don't worry because I am with you. Don't be afraid because I am your God. I will make you strong and will help you. I will support you with my right hand that saves you. ~ Isaiah 41:10

He was hated and rejected by people. He had much pain and suffering. People would not even look at him. He was hated, and we didn't even notice him. But he took our suffering on him and felt our pain for us. We saw his suffering. We thought God was punishing him. But he was wounded for the wrong things we did. He was crushed for the evil things we did. The punishment, which made us well, was given to him. And we are healed because of his wounds. ~ Isaiah 53:3-5

Those who go to God Most High for safety will be protected by God All-Powerful. I will say to the Lord, "You are my place of safety and protection. You are my God, and I trust you."

God will save you from hidden traps and from deadly diseases. He will protect you like a bird spreading its wings over its young. His truth will be like your armor and shield. You will not fear any danger by night or an arrow during the day. You will not be afraid of diseases that come in the dark or sickness that strikes at noon. At your side 1,000 people may die, or even 10,000 right beside you. But you will not be hurt. You will only watch what happens. You will see the wicked punished. The Lord is your protection. You have made God Most High your place of safety. Nothing bad will happen to you. No disaster will come to your home. He has put his angels in charge of you. They will watch over you wherever you go. They will catch you with their hands. And you will not hit your foot on a rock. You will walk on lions and cobras. You will step on strong lions and snakes. The Lord says, "If someone loves me, I will save him. I will protect those who know me. They will call to me, and I will answer them. I will be with them in trouble.

I will rescue them and honor them. I will give them a long, full life. They will see how I can save." Psalm 91

God gave the command and healed them. So they were saved from dying. ~ Psalm 107:20

I will bring back your health. And I will heal your injuries," says the Lord. ~ Jeremiah 30:17

Whatever you devise against the Lord, He will make a complete end of it. Distress will not rise up twice. ~ Nahum 1:9 NASB

And a man with leprosy came to Him and bowed down before Him, and said, "Lord, if You are willing, You can make me clean." Jesus reached out with His hand and touched him, saying, "I am willing; be cleansed." And immediately his leprosy was cleansed. Matthew 8:2-23 NASB

When Jesus came into Peter's home, He saw his mother-in-law lying sick in bed with a fever. And He touched her hand, and the fever left her; and she got up and waited on Him. Now when evening came, they brought to Him many who were demon-possessed; and He cast out the spirits with a word, and healed all who were ill. *This happened* so that what was spoken through

Isaiah the prophet would be fulfilled: "He Himself took our illnesses and carried away our diseases." Matthew 8:14-17 NASB

The thief comes only to steal and kill and destroy; I came so that they would have life, and have *it* abundantly. ~ John 10:10 NASB

Without becoming weak in faith he contemplated his own body, now *as good as* dead since he was about a hundred years old, and the deadness of Sarah's womb; yet, with respect to the promise of God, he did not waver in unbelief but grew strong in faith, giving glory to God, and being fully assured that what *God* had promised, He was able also to perform. Romans 4:19-21

But if the Spirit of Him who raised Jesus from the dead dwells in you, He who raised Christ Jesus from the dead will also give life to your mortal bodies through His Spirit who dwells in you. ~ Romans 8:11

God did not give us a spirit that makes us afraid but a spirit of power and love and self-control. 2 Tim 1:7 (NCV)

Let us hold firmly to the hope that we have confessed. We can trust God to do what he promised. Hebrews 10:23 (ICB)

Jesus Christ is the same yesterday, today, and forever. Hebrews 13:8 (ICB)

Christ carried our sins in his body on the cross. He did this so that we would stop living for sin and start living for what is right. And we are healed because of his wounds. 1 Peter 2:24 (ICB)

We can come to God with no doubts. This means that when we ask God for things (and those things agree with what God wants for us), then God cares about what we say. God listens to us every time we ask him. So, we know that he gives us the things that we ask from him.1 John 5:14-15 (ICB)

My dear friend, I know your soul is doing well. I pray that you are doing fine in every way and that your health is good. 3 John 2 (ICB)

But they overcame him by the blood of the Lamb and by the word of their testimony. Rev 12:11 (NET)

Confession:

Father, I know You are my Creator. I was created in Your image and in Your likeness. You know all about me.

Father, I thank You that You are the Lord, my Healer. You are the Lord, my Great Physician.

Thank You, Father, for doctors, nurses, and other healthcare professionals. But I put all my trust in You.

Father, You sent your Son, Jesus Christ, to the earth. You sent Him to die for all of humanity.

Father, You put sin and sickness on Jesus Christ when He was on the cross. Jesus took my sins and any sicknesses that may arise in my life.

While Jesus was on the earth, He healed multitudes of people.

Jesus looked at the multitude of people and had compassion for them. Jesus healed every one of them.

Jesus was made manifest to destroy all the works of the devil. Sickness is the work of the devil.

Jesus healed the blind, and they could see again with their eyes.

Jesus healed the lame, and they could walk again with their legs and feet.

Jesus healed the dumb, and they could speak and talk fluently.

Jesus healed fevers.

Jesus healed skin diseases.

Jesus raised a little girl from the dead.

Jesus healed a woman who was bent over, and she was made straight.

Jesus healed a woman who was so sick she spent all her money on doctor's bills. She made up her mind that when Jesus passed her way, she would touch His clothes. She was completely healed when she pressed through the crowds and touched the hem of Jesus' garment.

Jesus cast the devil out of men and women, restoring their right mind.

Everywhere Jesus went, He did good.

Jesus Christ is the same yesterday, today, and forever.

Because Jesus healed back then, He still heals today. He wants me completely well, all the time – free from sickness and disease.

Jesus, I thank You that You took and bore sicknesses and diseases so I don't have to. You took care of it forever -- so thank You.

Jesus is my healer and deliverer.

God's word is healing medicine.

When I read and meditate on God's word on healing, His word goes into my spirit and heals my body.

Thank You, Jesus!

A Child of God I am, amen!

[Note to parent: Lead your child in prayer based on this topic].

I BELIEVE IN MIRACLES

GOD'S WORD:

Below are accounts of some of the miracles of Jesus Christ. Read them and see the amazing miracles Jesus performed and believe Him for your miracle! All scripture references are NIV.

Jesus changed water into wine (John 2:1-11).

On the third day a wedding took place at Cana in Galilee. Jesus' mother was there, and Jesus and his disciples had also been invited to the wedding. When the wine was gone, Jesus' mother said to him, "They have no more wine." "Woman, why do you involve me?" Jesus replied. "My hour has not yet come." His mother said to the servants, "Do whatever he tells you." Nearby stood six stone water jars, the kind used by the Jews for ceremonial washing, each holding from twenty to thirty gallons. Jesus said to the servants, "Fill the jars with water" so they filled them to the brim. Then he told them, "Now draw some out and take it to the master of the banquet." They did so, and the master of the banquet tasted the water that had been turned into wine. He did not realize where it had come from, though the servants who had drawn the water knew. Then he called the bridegroom aside and said, "Everyone brings out the choice wine first and then the cheaper wine after the guests have had too much to drink; but you have saved the best till now." What Jesus did here in Cana of Galilee was the first of the signs through which he revealed his glory; and his disciples believed in him.

Jesus cured the nobleman's son (John 4:46-47).

Once more he visited Cana in Galilee, where he had turned the water into wine. And there was a certain royal official whose son lay sick at Capernaum. When this man heard that Jesus had arrived in Galilee from Judea, he went to him and begged him to come and heal his son, who was close to death.

The great catch of fishes (Luke 5:1-11).

One day as Jesus was standing by the Lake of Gennesaret, the people were crowding around him and listening to the word of God. He saw at the water's edge two boats, left there by the fishermen, who were washing their nets. He got into one of the boats, the one belonging to Simon, and asked him to put out a little from shore. Then he sat down and taught the people from the boat. When he had finished speaking, he said to Simon, "Put out into deep water, and let down the nets for a catch." Simon answered, "Master, we've worked hard all night and haven't caught anything. But because you say so, I will let down the nets." When they had done so, they caught such a large number of fish that their nets began to break. So they signaled their partners in the other boat to come and help them, and they came and filled both boats so full that they began to sink. When Simon Peter saw this, he fell at Jesus' knees and said, "Go away from me, Lord; I am a sinful man!" For he and all his companions were astonished at the catch of fish they had taken, and so were James and John, the sons of Zebedee, Simon's partners. Then Jesus said to Simon, "Don't be afraid; from now on you will fish for people." So they pulled their boats up on shore, left everything and followed him.

Jesus cast out an unclean spirit (<u>Mark 1:23-28</u>).

Just then a man in their synagogue who was possessed by an impure spirit cried out, "What do you want with us, Jesus of Nazareth? Have you come to destroy us? I know who you are—the Holy One of God!" "Be quiet!" said Jesus sternly. "Come out of him!" The impure spirit shook the man violently and came out of him with a shriek. The people were all so amazed that they asked each other, "What is this? A new teaching—and with authority! He even gives orders to impure spirits and they obey him." News about him spread quickly over the whole region of Galilee.

Jesus cured Peter's mother-in-law of a fever (<u>Mark 1:30-31</u>).

Simon's mother-in-law was in bed with a fever, and they immediately told Jesus about her. So, he went to her, took her hand, and helped her up. The fever left her, and she began to wait on them.

Jesus healed a leper (<u>Mark 1:40-45</u>).

A man with leprosy came to him and begged him on his knees, "If you are willing, you can make me clean." Jesus was indignant. He reached out his hand and touched the man. "I am willing," he said. "Be clean!" Immediately the leprosy left him, and he was cleansed. Jesus sent him away at once with a strong warning: "See that you don't tell this to anyone. But go, show yourself to the priest and offer the sacrifices that Moses commanded for your cleansing, as a testimony to them." Instead, he went out and began to talk freely, spreading the news. As a result, Jesus could no longer enter a town openly but stayed outside in lonely places. Yet the people still came to him from everywhere.

Jesus healed the centurion's servant (<u>Matthew 8:5-13</u>).

When Jesus had entered Capernaum, a centurion came to him, asking for help. "Lord," he said, "my servant lies at home paralyzed, suffering terribly." Jesus said to him, "Shall I come and heal him?" The centurion replied, "Lord, I do not deserve to have you come under my roof. But just say the word, and my servant will be healed. For I myself am a man under authority, with soldiers under me. I tell this one, 'Go,' and he goes; and that one, 'Come,' and he comes. I say to my servant, 'Do this,' and he does it." When Jesus heard this, he was amazed and said to those following him, "Truly I tell you, I have not found anyone in Israel with such great faith. I say to you that many will come from the east and the west and will take their places at the feast with Abraham, Isaac, and Jacob in the kingdom of heaven. But the subjects of the kingdom will be thrown outside, into the darkness, where there will be weeping and gnashing of teeth." Then Jesus said to the centurion, "Go! Let it be done just as you believed it would." And his servant was healed at that moment.

Jesus raised the widow's son from the dead (Luke 7:11-18).

Soon afterward, Jesus went to a town called Nain, and his disciples and a large crowd went along with him. As he approached the town gate, a dead person was being carried out—the only son of his mother, and she was a widow. And a large crowd from the town was with her. When the Lord saw her, his heart went out to her and he said, "Don't cry." Then he went up and touched the bier they were carrying him on, and the bearers stood still. He said, "Young man, I say to you, get up!" The dead man sat up and began to talk, and Jesus gave him back to his mother. They were all filled with awe and praised God. "A great prophet has appeared among us," they said. "God has come to help his people." This news about Jesus spread throughout Judea and the surrounding country. John's disciples told him about all these things.

Jesus cured a woman of an issue of blood (Luke 8:43-48).

And a woman was there who had been subject to bleeding for twelve years, but no one could heal her. She came up behind him and touched the edge of his cloak, and immediately her bleeding stopped. "Who touched me?" Jesus asked. When they all denied it, Peter said, "Master, the people are crowding and pressing against you." But Jesus said, "Someone touched me; I know that power has gone out from me." Then the woman, seeing that she could not go unnoticed, came trembling and fell at his feet. In the presence of all the people, she told why she had touched him and how she had been instantly healed. Then he said to her, "Daughter, your faith has healed you. Go in peace."

Jesus opened the eyes of two blind men (<u>Matthew 9:27-31</u>).

As Jesus went on from there, two blind men followed him, calling out, "Have mercy on us, Son of David!" When he had gone indoors, the blind men came to him, and he asked them, "Do you believe that I am able to do this?" "Yes, Lord," they replied. Then he touched their eyes and said, "According to your faith let it be done to you"; and their sight was restored. Jesus warned them sternly, "See that no one knows about this." But they went out and spread the news about him all over that region.

Jesus loosened the tongue of a man who could not speak (<u>Matthew 9:32-33</u>).

While they were going out, a man who was demon-possessed and could not talk was brought to Jesus. And when the demon was driven out, the man who had been mute spoke. The crowd was amazed and said, "Nothing like this has ever been seen in Israel."

Jesus healed an invalid man at the pool called Bethesda (<u>John 5:1-9</u>).

Sometime later, Jesus went up to Jerusalem for one of the Jewish festivals. Now there is in Jerusalem near the Sheep Gate a pool, which in Aramaic is called Bethesda and which is surrounded by five covered colonnades. Here a great number of disabled people used to lie—the blind, the lame, the paralyzed. One who was there had been an invalid for thirty-eight years. When Jesus saw him lying there and learned that he had been in this condition for a long time, he asked him, "Do you want to get well?" "Sir," the invalid replied, "I have no one to help me into the pool when the water is stirred. While I am trying to get in, someone else goes down ahead of me." Then Jesus said to him, "Get up! Pick up your mat and walk." At once the man was cured; he picked up his mat and walked. The day on which this took place was a Sabbath.

Jesus stilled the storm (<u>Matthew 8:23-27</u>).

Then he got into the boat and his disciples followed him. Suddenly a furious storm came up on the lake so that the waves swept over the boat. But Jesus was sleeping. The disciples went and woke him, saying, "Lord, save us! We're going to drown!" He replied, "You of little faith, why are you so afraid?" Then he got up and rebuked the winds and the waves, and it was completely calm. The men were amazed and asked, "What kind of man is this? Even the winds and the waves obey him!"

Jesus cured two demoniacs (<u>Matthew 8:28-34</u>).

When he arrived at the other side in the region of the Gadarenes, two demon-possessed men coming from the tombs met him. They were so violent that no one could pass that way. "What do you want with us, Son of God?" they shouted. "Have you come here to torture us before the appointed time?" Some distance from them a large herd of pigs was feeding. The demons begged Jesus, "If you drive us out, send us into the herd of pigs." He said to them, "Go!" So, they came out and went into the pigs, and the whole herd rushed down the steep bank into the lake and died in the water. Those tending the pigs ran off, went into the town, and reported all this, including what had happened to the demon-possessed men. Then the whole town went out to meet Jesus. And when they saw him, they pleaded with him to leave their region.

Jesus cured the paralytic (<u>Matthew 9:1-8</u>).

Jesus stepped into a boat, crossed over and came to his own town. Some men brought to him a paralyzed man, lying on a mat. When Jesus saw their faith, he said to the man, "Take heart, son; your sins are forgiven." At this, some of the teachers of the law said to themselves, "This fellow is blaspheming!" Knowing their thoughts, Jesus said, "Why do you entertain evil thoughts in your hearts? Which is easier: to say, 'Your sins are forgiven,' or to say, 'Get up and walk'? But I want you to know that the Son of Man has authority on earth to forgive sins." So, he said to the paralyzed man, "Get up, take your mat and go home." Then the man got up and went home. When the crowd saw this, they were filled with awe; and they praised God, who had given such authority to man.

Jesus raised the ruler's daughter from the dead (<u>Matthew 9:18-26</u>).

While he was saying this, a synagogue leader came and knelt before him and said, "My daughter has just died. But come and put your hand on her, and she will live." Jesus got up and went with him, and so did his disciples. Just then a woman who had been subject to bleeding for twelve years came up behind him and touched the edge of his cloak. She said to herself, "If I only touch his cloak, I will be healed." Jesus turned and saw her. "Take heart, daughter," he said, "your faith has healed you." And the woman was healed at that moment. When Jesus entered the synagogue leader's house and saw the noisy crowd and people playing pipes, he said, "Go away. The girl is not dead but asleep." But they laughed at him. After the crowd had been put outside, he went in and took the girl by the hand, and she got up. News of this spread through all that region.

Jesus restored a withered hand (<u>Matthew 12:10-13</u>).

And a man with a shriveled hand was there. Looking for a reason to bring charges against Jesus, they asked him, "Is it lawful to heal on the Sabbath?" He said to them, "If any of you has a sheep and it falls into a pit on the Sabbath, will you not take hold of it and lift it out? How much more valuable is a person than a sheep! Therefore, it is lawful to do good on the Sabbath." Then he said to the man, "Stretch out your hand." So, he stretched it out and it was completely restored, just as sound as the other.

Jesus cured a demon-possessed man (<u>Matthew 12:22</u>).

Then they brought him a demon-possessed man who was blind and mute, and Jesus healed him, so that he could both talk and see.

Jesus fed at least five thousand people (<u>Matthew 14:15-21</u>).

As evening approached, the disciples came to him and said, "This is a remote place, and it's already getting late. Send the crowds away, so they can go to the villages and buy themselves some food." Jesus replied, "They do not need to go away. You give them something to eat." "We have here only five loaves of bread and two fish," they answered. "Bring them here to me," he said. And he directed the people to sit down on the grass. Taking the five loaves and the two fish and looking up to heaven, he gave thanks and broke the loaves. Then he gave them to the disciples, and the disciples gave them to the people. They all ate and were satisfied, and the disciples picked up twelve basketfuls of broken pieces that were left over. The number of those who ate was about five thousand men, besides women and children.

Jesus healed a woman of Canaan (<u>Matthew 15:22-28</u>).

A Canaanite woman from that vicinity came to him, crying out, "Lord, Son of David, have mercy on me! My daughter is demon-possessed and suffering terribly." Jesus did not answer a word. So, his disciples came to him and urged him, "Send her away, for she keeps crying out after us." He answered, "I was sent only to the lost sheep of Israel." The woman came and knelt before him. "Lord, help me!" she said. He replied, "It is not right to take the children's bread and toss it to the dogs." "Yes, it is, Lord," she said. "Even the dogs eat the crumbs that fall from their master's table." Then Jesus said to her, "Woman, you have great faith! Your request is granted." And her daughter was healed at that moment.

Jesus cured a deaf and mute man (<u>Mark 7:31-37</u>).

Then Jesus left the vicinity of Tyre and went through Sidon, down to the Sea of Galilee and into the region of the Decapolis. There some people brought to him a man who was deaf and could hardly talk, and they begged Jesus to place his hand on him. After he took him aside, away from the crowd, Jesus put his fingers into the man's ears. Then he spit and touched the man's tongue. He looked up to heaven and with a deep sigh said to him, "Ephphatha!" (which means "Be opened!"). At this, the man's ears were opened, his tongue was loosened, and he began to speak plainly. Jesus commanded them not to tell anyone. But the more he did so, the more they kept talking about it. People were overwhelmed with amazement. "He has done everything well," they said. "He even makes the deaf hear and the mute speak."

Jesus fed over four thousand people (<u>Matthew 15:32-39</u>).

Jesus called his disciples to him and said, "I have compassion for these people; they have already been with me three days and have nothing to eat. I do not want to send them away hungry, or they may collapse on the way." His disciples answered, "Where could we get enough bread in this remote place to feed such a crowd?" "How many loaves do you have?" Jesus asked. "Seven," they replied, "and a few small fish." He told the crowd to sit down on the ground. Then he took the seven loaves and the fish, and when he had given thanks, he broke them and gave them to the disciples, and they in turn to the people. They all ate and were satisfied. Afterward the disciples picked up seven basketfuls of broken pieces that were left over. The number of those who ate was four thousand men, besides women and children. After Jesus had sent the crowd away, he got into the boat and went to the vicinity of Magadan.

Jesus opened the eyes of a blind man (<u>Mark 8:22-26</u>).

They came to Bethsaida, and some people brought a blind man and begged Jesus to touch him. He took the blind man by the hand and led him outside the village. When he had spit on the man's eyes and put his hands on him, Jesus asked, "Do you see anything?" He looked up and said, "I see people; they look like trees walking around." Once more Jesus put his hands on the man's eyes. Then his eyes were opened, his sight was restored, and he saw everything clearly. Jesus sent him home, saying, "Don't even go into the village."

Jesus cured a boy who was plagued by a demon (<u>Matthew 17:14-21</u>).

When they came to the crowd, a man approached Jesus and knelt before him. "Lord, have mercy on my son," he said. "He has seizures and is suffering greatly. He often falls into the fire or into the water. I brought him to your disciples, but they could not heal him." "You unbelieving and perverse generation," Jesus replied, "how long shall I stay with you? How long shall I put up with you? Bring the boy here to me." Jesus rebuked the demon, and it came out of the boy, and he was healed at that moment. Then the disciples came to Jesus in private and asked, "Why couldn't we drive it out?" He replied, "Because you have so little faith. Truly I tell you, if you have faith as small as a mustard seed, you can say to this mountain, 'Move from here to there,' and it will move. Nothing will be impossible for you."

Jesus opened the eyes of a man born blind (<u>John 9:1-38</u>)

As he went along, he saw a man blind from birth. His disciples asked him, "Rabbi, who sinned, this man or his parents, that he was born blind?" "Neither this man nor his parents sinned," said Jesus, "but this happened so that the works of God might be displayed in him. As long as it is day, we must do the works of him who sent me. Night is coming, when no one can work. While I am in the world, I am the light of the world." After saying this, he spit on the ground, made some mud with the saliva, and put it on the man's eyes. "Go," he told him, "wash in the Pool of Siloam" (this word means "Sent"). So the man went and washed, and came home seeing. His neighbors and those who had formerly seen him begging asked, "Isn't this the same man who used to sit and beg?" Some claimed that he was. Others said, "No, he only looks like him." But he himself insisted, "I am the man." "How then were your eyes opened?" they asked. He replied, "The man they call Jesus made some mud and put it on my eyes. He told me to go to Siloam and wash. So I went and washed, and then I could see." "Where is this man?" they asked him. "I don't know," he said. They brought to the Pharisees the man who had been blind. Now the day on which Jesus had made the mud and opened the man's eyes was the Sabbath. Therefore, the Pharisees also asked him how he had received his sight. "He put mud on my eyes," the man replied, "and I washed, and now I see." Some of the Pharisees said, "This man is not from God, for he does not keep the Sabbath." But others asked, "How can a sinner perform such signs?" So, they were divided. Then they turned again to the blind man, "What have you to say about him? It was your eyes he opened." The man replied, "He is a prophet." They still did not believe that he had been blind and had received his sight until they sent for the man's parents. "Is this your son?" they asked. "Is this the one you say was born blind? How is it that now he can see?" "We know he is our son," the parents answered, "and we know he was born blind. But how he can see now, or who opened his eyes, we don't know. Ask him. He is of age; he will speak for himself." His parents said this because they were afraid of the Jewish leaders, who already had decided that anyone who acknowledged that Jesus was the Messiah would be put out of the synagogue. That was why his parents said, "He is of age; ask him." A second time they summoned the man who had been blind. "Give glory to God by telling the truth," they said. "We know this man is a sinner." He replied, "Whether he is a sinner or not, I don't know. One thing I do know. I was blind but now I see!" Then they asked him, "What did he do to you? How did he open your eyes?" He answered, "I have told you already and you did not listen. Why do you want to hear it again? Do you want to become his disciples too?" Then they hurled insults at him and said, "You are this fellow's disciple! We are disciples of Moses! We know that God spoke to Moses, but as for this fellow, we don't even know where he comes from." The man answered, "Now that is remarkable! You don't know where he comes from, yet he opened my eyes. We know that God does not listen to sinners. He listens to the godly person who does his will. Nobody has ever heard of opening the eyes of a man born blind. If this man were not from God, he could do nothing." To this, they replied, "You were steeped in sin at birth; how dare you lecture us!" And they threw him out. Jesus heard that they had thrown him out, and when he found him, he said, "Do you believe in the Son of Man?" "Who is he, sir?" the man asked. "Tell me so that I may believe in him." Jesus said, "You have now seen him; in fact, he is the one speaking with you." Then the man said, "Lord, I believe," and he worshiped him.

Jesus cured a woman who had been afflicted for eighteen years (<u>Luke 13:10-17</u>).

On a Sabbath, Jesus was teaching in one of the synagogues, and a woman was there who had been crippled by a spirit for eighteen years. She was bent over and could not straighten up at all. When Jesus saw her, he called her forward and said to her, "Woman, you are set free from your infirmity." Then he put his hands on her, and immediately she straightened up and praised God. Indignant because Jesus had healed on the Sabbath, the synagogue leader said to the people, "There are six days for work. So come and be healed on those days, not on the Sabbath." The Lord answered him, "You hypocrites! Doesn't each of you on the Sabbath untie your ox or donkey from the stall and lead it out to give it water? Then should not this woman, a daughter of Abraham, whom Satan has kept bound for eighteen long years, be set free on the Sabbath day from what bound her?" When he said this, all his opponents were humiliated, but the people were delighted with all the wonderful things he was doing.

Jesus cured a man of dropsy (Luke 14:1-4).

One Sabbath, when Jesus went to eat in the house of a prominent Pharisee, he was being carefully watched. There in front of him was a man suffering from abnormal swelling of his body. Jesus asked the Pharisees and experts in the law, "Is it lawful to heal on the Sabbath or not?" But they remained silent. So taking hold of the man, he healed him and sent him on his way.

Jesus cleansed ten lepers (Luke 17:11-19).

Now on his way to Jerusalem, Jesus traveled along the border between Samaria and Galilee. As he was going into a village, ten men who had leprosy met him. They stood at a distance and called out in a loud voice, "Jesus, Master, have pity on us!" When he saw them, he said, "Go, show yourselves to the priests." And as they went, they were cleansed. One of them, when he saw he was healed, came back, praising God in a loud voice. He threw himself at Jesus' feet and thanked him—and he was a Samaritan. Jesus asked, "Were not all ten cleansed? Where are the other nine? Has no one returned to give praise to God except this foreigner?" Then he said to him, "Rise and go; your faith has made you well."

Jesus raised Lazarus from the dead (John 11:1-46).

Now a man named Lazarus was sick. He was from Bethany, the village of Mary, and her sister Martha. (This Mary, whose brother Lazarus now lay sick, was the same one who poured perfume on the Lord and wiped his feet with her hair.) So, the sisters sent word to Jesus, "Lord, the one you love is sick." When he heard this, Jesus said, "This sickness will not end in death. No, it is for God's glory so that God's Son may be glorified through it." Now Jesus loved Martha and her sister and Lazarus. So, when he heard that Lazarus was sick, he stayed where he was two more days, and then he said to his disciples, "Let us go back to Judea." "But Rabbi," they said, "a short while ago the Jews there tried to stone you, and yet you are going back?" Jesus answered, "Are there not twelve hours of daylight? Anyone who walks in the daytime will not stumble, for they see by this world's light. It is when a person walks at night that they stumble, for they have no light." After he had said this, he went on to tell them, "Our friend Lazarus has fallen asleep; but I am going there to wake him up." His disciples replied, "Lord, if he sleeps, he will get better." Jesus had been speaking of his death, but his disciples thought he meant natural sleep. So, then he told them plainly, "Lazarus is dead, and for your sake I am glad I was not there, so that you may believe. But let us go to him." Then Thomas (also known as Didymus) said to the rest of the disciples, "Let us also go, that we may die with him."

On his arrival, Jesus found that Lazarus had already been in the tomb for four days. Now Bethany was less than two miles from Jerusalem, and many Jews had come to Martha and Mary to comfort them in the loss of their brother. When Martha heard that Jesus was coming, she went out to meet him, but Mary stayed at home. "Lord," Martha said to Jesus, "if you had been here, my brother would not have died. But I know that even now God will give you whatever you ask." Jesus said to her, "Your brother will rise again." Martha answered, "I know he will rise again in the resurrection at the last day." Jesus said to her, "I am the resurrection and the life. The one who believes in me will live, even though they die; and whoever lives by believing in me will never die. Do you believe this?" "Yes, Lord," she replied, "I believe that you are the Messiah, the Son of God, who is to come into the world." After she had said this, she went back and called her sister Mary aside. "The Teacher is here," she said, "and is asking for you." When Mary heard this, she got up quickly and went to him. Now Jesus had not yet entered the village, but was still at the place where Martha had met him. When the Jews who had been with Mary in the house, comforting her, noticed how quickly she got up and went out, they followed her, supposing she was going to the tomb to mourn there. When Mary reached the place where Jesus was and saw him, she fell at his feet and said, "Lord, if you had been here, my brother would not have died." When Jesus saw her weeping, and the Jews who had come along with her also weeping, he was deeply moved in spirit and troubled. "Where have you laid him?" he asked. "Come and see, Lord," they replied. Jesus wept. Then the Jews said, "See how he loved him!" But some of them said, "Could not he who opened the eyes of the blind man have kept this man from dying?

Jesus, once more deeply moved, came to the tomb. It was a cave with a stone laid across the entrance. "Take away the stone," he said. "But, Lord," said Martha, the sister of the dead man, "by this time there is a bad odor, for he has been there four days." Then Jesus said, "Did I not tell you that if you believe, you will see the glory of God?" So they took away the stone. Then Jesus looked up and said, "Father, I thank you that you have heard me. I knew that you always hear me, but I said this for the benefit of the people standing here, that they may believe that you sent me." When he had said this, Jesus called in a loud voice, "Lazarus, come out!" The dead man came out, his hands and feet wrapped with strips of linen, and a cloth around his face. Jesus said to them, "Take off the grave clothes and let him go."

Therefore, many of the Jews who had come to visit Mary, and had seen what Jesus did, believed in him. But some of them went to the Pharisees and told them what Jesus had done.

Jesus opened the eyes of two blind men (<u>Matthew 20:30-34</u>).

Two blind men were sitting by the roadside, and when they heard that Jesus was going by, they shouted, "Lord, Son of David, have mercy on us!" The crowd rebuked them and told them to be quiet, but they shouted all the louder, "Lord, Son of David, have mercy on us!" Jesus stopped and called them. "What do you want me to do for you?" he asked. "Lord," they answered, "we want our sight." Jesus had compassion on them and touched their eyes. Immediately they received their sight and followed him.

Jesus caused the fig tree to wither (Matthew 21:18-22).

Early in the morning, as Jesus was on his way back to the city, he was hungry. Seeing a fig tree by the road, he went up to it but found nothing on it except leaves. Then he said to it, "May you never bear fruit again!" Immediately the tree withered. When the disciples saw this, they were amazed. "How did the fig tree wither so quickly?" they asked. Jesus replied, "Truly I tell you, if you have faith and do not doubt, not only can you do what was done to the fig tree, but also you can say to this mountain, 'Go, throw yourself into the sea,' and it will be done. If you believe, you will receive whatever you ask for in prayer."

Jesus restored the ear of the high priest's servant (Luke 22:50-51).

And one of them struck the servant of the high priest, cutting off his right ear. But Jesus answered, "No more of this!" And he touched the man's ear and healed him.

Jesus rose from the dead (Luke 24:5-8).

In their fright, the women bowed down with their faces to the ground, but the men said to them, "Why do you look for the living among the dead? He is not here; he has risen! Remember how he told you, while he was still with you in Galilee: 'The Son of Man must be delivered over to the hands of sinners, be crucified, and on the third day be raised again.'" Then they remembered his words.

The second great haul of fishes (John 21:1-14).

Afterward, Jesus appeared again to his disciples, by the Sea of Galilee. It happened this way: Simon Peter, Thomas (also known as Didymus), Nathanael from Cana in Galilee, the sons of Zebedee, and two other disciples were together. "I'm going out to fish," Simon Peter told them, and they said, "We'll go with you." So, they went out and got into the boat, but that night they caught nothing. Early in the morning, Jesus stood on the shore, but the disciples did not realize that it was Jesus. He called out to them, "Friends, haven't you any fish?" No," they answered. He said, "Throw your net on the right side of the boat and you will find some." When they did, they were unable to haul the net in because of the large number of fish. Then the disciple whom Jesus loved said to Peter, "It is the Lord!" As soon as Simon Peter heard him say, "It is the Lord," he wrapped his outer garment around him (for he had taken it off) and jumped into the water. The other disciples followed in the boat, towing the net full of fish, for they were not far from shore, about a hundred yards. When they landed, they saw a fire of burning coals there with fish on it, and some bread. Jesus said to them, "Bring some of the fish you have just caught." So Simon Peter climbed back into the boat and dragged the net ashore. It was full of large fish, but even with so many the net was not torn. Jesus said to them, "Come and have breakfast." None of the disciples dared ask him, "Who are you?" They knew it was the Lord. Jesus came, took the bread and gave it to them, and did the same with the fish. This was now the third time Jesus appeared to his disciples after he was raised from the dead.

CONFESSION:

I believe in miracles!

I believe Jesus wants everyone healed and whole.

Everywhere Jesus went, He was doing good. Jesus showed compassion for people – healing the sick, raising the dead, feeding the hungry, and delivering people from demons.

Jesus was -- and still is -- anointed to do miracles!

A miracle is the supernatural power of God.

Miracles still happen today!

Miracles show God's love for people.

Miracles show God's mercy and His kindness.

Sickness is of the devil.

Miracles are from God.

God wants to show His love and mercy towards me and every human being.

All I need to do is believe!

All through the Word of God, Jesus did miracles.

He was and is always loving and wants all people healed from the devil's oppression.

And Jesus is the same as He was yesterday, today, and forever!

What Jesus did long ago, He still does today.

Today, God works through His people to perform His miracles. All God needs is faith in Him and His Word.

A Child of God I am, amen!

[Note to parent: Lead your child in prayer based on this topic].

GOD WILL DELIVER ME!

GOD'S WORD:

> **The Deliverance from the Fiery Furnace, Daniel 3**
> **(NIV)**

King Nebuchadnezzar made an image of gold, sixty cubits high and six cubits wide, and set it up on the plain of Dura in the province of Babylon. He then summoned the satraps, prefects, governors, advisers, treasurers, judges, magistrates and all the other provincial officials to come to the dedication of the image he had set up. So the satraps, prefects, governors, advisers, treasurers, judges, magistrates and all the other provincial officials assembled for the dedication of the image that King Nebuchadnezzar had set up, and they stood before it. Then the herald loudly proclaimed, "Nations and peoples of every language, this is what you are commanded to do: As soon as you hear the sound of the horn, flute, zither, lyre, harp, pipe and all kinds of music, you must fall down and worship the image of gold that King Nebuchadnezzar has set up. Whoever does not fall down, and worship will immediately be thrown into a blazing furnace." Therefore, as soon as they heard the sound of the horn, flute, zither, lyre, harp and all kinds of music, all the nations and peoples of every language fell down and worshiped the image of gold that King Nebuchadnezzar had set up.

At this time some astrologers came forward and denounced the Jews. They said to King Nebuchadnezzar, "May the king live forever! Your Majesty has issued a decree that everyone who hears the sound of the horn, flute, zither, lyre, harp, pipe and all kinds of music must fall down and worship the image of gold, and that whoever does not fall down and worship will be thrown into a blazing furnace. But there are some Jews whom you have set over the affairs of the province of Babylon-Shadrach, Meshach and Abednego-who pay no attention to you, Your Majesty. They neither serve your gods nor worship the image of gold you have set up." Furious with rage, Nebuchadnezzar summoned Shadrach, Meshach and Abednego. So these men were brought before the king, and Nebuchadnezzar said to them, "Is it true, Shadrach, Meshach and Abednego, that you do not serve my gods or worship the image of gold I have set up? Now when you hear the sound of the horn, flute, zither, lyre, harp, pipe and all kinds of music, if you are ready to fall down and worship the image I made, very good. But if you do not worship it, you will be thrown immediately into a blazing furnace. Then what god will be able to rescue you from my hand?" Shadrach, Meshach and Abednego replied to him, "King Nebuchadnezzar, we do not need to defend ourselves before you in this matter. If we are thrown into the blazing furnace, the God we serve is able to deliver us from it, and he will deliver us from Your Majesty's hand. But even if he does not, we want you to know, Your Majesty, that we will not serve your gods or worship the image of gold you have set up."

Then Nebuchadnezzar was furious with Shadrach, Meshach and Abednego, and his attitude toward them changed. He ordered the furnace heated seven times hotter than usual and commanded some of the strongest soldiers in his army to tie up Shadrach, Meshach and Abednego and throw them into the blazing furnace. So these men, wearing their robes, trousers, turbans and other clothes, were bound and thrown into the blazing furnace. The king's command was so urgent and the furnace so hot that the flames of the fire killed the soldiers who took up Shadrach, Meshach and Abednego, and these three men, firmly tied, fell into the blazing furnace. Then King Nebuchadnezzar leaped to his feet in amazement and asked his advisers, "Weren't there three men that we tied up and threw into the fire?" They replied, "Certainly, Your Majesty." He said, "Look! I see four men walking around in the fire, unbound and unharmed, and the fourth looks like a son of the gods." Nebuchadnezzar then approached the opening of the blazing furnace and shouted, "Shadrach, Meshach and Abednego, servants of the Most High God, come out! Come here!" So, Shadrach, Meshach and Abednego came out of the fire, and the satraps, prefects, governors and royal advisers crowded around them. They saw that the fire had not harmed their bodies, nor was a hair of their heads singed; their robes were not scorched, and there was no smell of fire on them.

Then Nebuchadnezzar said, "Praise be to the God of Shadrach, Meshach and Abednego, who has sent his angel and rescued his servants! They trusted in him and defied the king's command and were willing to give up their lives rather than serve or worship any god except their own God. Therefore, I decree that the people of any nation or language who say anything against the God of Shadrach, Meshach and Abednego be cut into pieces and their houses be turned into piles of rubble, for no other god can save in this way." Then the king promoted Shadrach, Meshach and Abednego in the province of Babylon.

CONFESSION:

I am like the three Hebrews who love God with all their heart.

I will not bow or give in to the enemy's suggestions.

I will not be moved by my peers who try to test my love for God.

I choose to love and serve God with all my heart.

I will be true to God.

God loves and cares for me. God provides and protects me.

God is faithful to His word.

If ever I am being forced to deny God's love or if anyone tries to persuade me to serve the devil, I will not bow. I will stand my ground and choose God every time.

Just like God delivered the three Hebrews from the burning fiery furnace, God will deliver me from every trap that the enemy sets.

God is pleased when I have faith in Him. He will reward me every time because I believe in Him.

Just like the three Hebrews who came out of the burning, fiery furnace – I, too will experience the mighty hand of God's deliverance for me.

A Child of God, I am!

[Note to parent: Lead your child in prayer based on this topic].

A GUIDE FOR PARENTS

TEACHING ON THE HOLY SPIRIT

(Explained so that a child can grasp and understand)

Who is the Holy Spirit?

The Holy Spirit is part of the true and living God. It's like how you might have different team parts, and they're all equally important. So, there's God the Father, God the Son (Jesus), and God the Holy Spirit. Even though it's hard to understand fully, the Holy Spirit helps us explain this to kids. We believe this because it's in the Bible (2 Cor. 13:14). People often use the word "trinity" to talk about God being three in one.

What does the Holy Spirit do?

The Holy Spirit was also there when the world was made, along with God the Father and Jesus. In the very beginning, the Spirit was hovering over the waters (Genesis 1:2). There's a part in the Bible where a person named Job says, "The Spirit of God made me" (Job 33:4). The Holy Spirit authored the Bible through men, so we could understand what God wants us to know. The Holy Spirit ~ is the Spirit of Truth (John 16:13-14; 2 Pet. 1:21) that talks to us and helps us understand why we need Jesus.

How does the Holy Spirit help us every day?

The Holy Spirit does different things to help us. He's our Helper, Convictor, Guide, Teacher, and a Changer.

- Every day, the Holy Spirit helps us do things that make God happy (Phil. 2:13).

- If we do something wrong, the Holy Spirit makes us feel bad inside (John 16:8). This helps us know we need to apologize to God, who promises to forgive us (1 John 1:9).

- The Holy Spirit shows us how to live in a good way for God (Rom. 8:14; John 16:13). We learn this by reading the Bible and praying.

- The Bible is really the Holy Spirit explaining things about God (John 14:16). It's like having a personal teacher!

- The Holy Spirit changes us to be more like Jesus (Gal. 5:22-23). God forgives our mistakes and fills our hearts with good things!

About the Holy Spirit's baptism

Sometimes, kids might feel a bit worried when they see the Holy Spirit moving in church, especially if they're shy or don't quite understand what's going on in a service or any setting where the presence of God is present. Parents, teachers, and pastors should help them understand what's happening. We can tell if it's the Holy Spirit or our emotions. Kids should know that being baptized by the Holy Spirit is a wonderful gift from God, and we don't need to fear it (1 John 4:16-18).

It's important to know that the Holy Spirit's baptism isn't just for grown-ups; it's for everyone who believes, including kids! We should teach kids that they're made in God's image and can have a special connection with Him. We should also explain that becoming a Christian and being baptized in the Holy Spirit are different things. Even though all believers have the Holy Spirit, being baptized in the Spirit is a unique experience. The Bible says this gift is available to all believers, even now (1 John 4:13; Romans 4:18; Acts 19:1-6; Acts 2:38).

Getting the Holy Spirit's baptism is like receiving a super special present; kids don't need to worry about memorizing things or following specific rules. As they try to get closer to God and live with the Holy Spirit's help, they will speak in a special way called "tongues." This is a gift from God that He gives us because He loves us a lot. Like any present, God gives the Holy Spirit freely because He loves His kids and wants them to be full of His Spirit (Acts 1:4-8; Luke 11:13).

How can we pray for the Holy Spirit?

To start, read this part of the Bible together as a family:

Luke 11:9-10, 13: Jesus said, "So I say to you: Ask and it will be given to you; seek and you will find; knock and the door will be opened to you. For everyone who asks receives; the one who seeks finds; and to the one who knocks, the door will be opened...how much more will your heavenly Father give the Holy Spirit to those who ask Him."

If you want to get the Holy Spirit's baptism, you can pray this way:

Dear Jesus,

You promised in the Bible that we can have the Holy Spirit. I want to have the Holy Spirit in my life. Please help me be filled with the Holy Spirit as You did for the disciples. I love You and want to live the way You want me to. Thank You for loving me. Amen.

When kids receive the Holy Spirit's baptism, they will start speaking in tongues. If they feel like the Holy Spirit is giving them words, they can say them out loud. It is important to show they trust God and want His special gift.

As you pray with your child, remember these things to help them understand the Holy Spirit better:

1. Let your child **want** to talk to Jesus. Don't make them do it if they don't want to. When they're ready, pray together.

2. Listen to what they want to talk to Jesus about. Sometimes, they might need help with other things more urgently. Pray for those things first, then ask for the Holy Spirit's gift.

3. Jesus is the One who gives the Holy Spirit. You can't make it happen faster. So, be patient and know that Jesus knows the best time. You're there to support and encourage your child.

4. Show them lots of love. If your child doesn't get the Holy Spirit's baptism right away, be there to show them love and support. Keep praying and seeking if it takes some time (Luke 11:13).

CALL TO SALVATION

GOD'S WORD:

God loves you

1 John 4:10 "True love is God's love for us, not our love for God. God sent his Son to die in our place to take away our sins."

Sin separates us from God

Romans 6:23 "The payment for sin is death. But God gives us the free gift of life forever in Christ Jesus our Lord." (ICB)

Christ died for us

Romans 5:8 "But Christ died for us while we were still sinners. In this way God shows his great love for us." (ICB)

Everyone sins

Romans 3:23 "All people have sinned and are not good enough for God's glory."

Confess and ask for forgiveness for sin

1 John 1:9 "But if we confess our sins, he will forgive our sins. We can trust God. He does what is right. He will make us clean from all the wrongs we have done." (ICB)

Believe and be saved

Acts 16:31 They replied, "Believe in the Lord Jesus, and you will be saved—you and your household." (NIV)

Follow Jesus

Romans 10:9 "If you declare with your mouth, "Jesus is Lord," and believe in your heart that God raised him from the dead, you will be saved. (NIV)

LEADING YOUR CHILD TO JESUS/CALL TO SALVATION:

When your child is ready to invite Jesus into their life, it's essential to explain the salvation story in a way they can understand. Here's a sample script you can use or adapt to talk and pray with your child:

The salvation story:

The Bible tells us that God created the world, and it was perfect. However, because of Satan's lies and temptation, Adam and Eve sinned, bringing sin, sickness, and death into the world. We all make mistakes that move us away from God, and the punishment for sin is death.

But don't worry, because God loves the whole world so much, including you and me! He loved us so much that He sent His only son, Jesus, to die on the cross as payment for our sins. When we tell Jesus about our mistakes, ask Him for forgiveness, and invite Him to be the leader of our lives, He is faithful to forgive us. Then, we get to be best friends with Jesus forever, both here on earth and in heaven. We'll always be connected to Jesus, no matter what happens.

Salvation prayer example:

I usually ask the child to repeat this prayer after me. After we pray, let's celebrate! Share the great news with everyone you know. Let your child tell them the wonderful decision they've made. Celebrate by having their favorite food for dinner. This is a huge deal; you'll want your child to remember this special moment joyfully.

"Dear God,

Thank You for loving me so much that You sent Your son, Jesus, to die on the cross for my sins. I'm sorry for the wrong things I've done. Please cleanse my heart and forgive me. I want to be best friends with You forever. Please show me how to listen to and follow You every day. Thank You for always being with me. I love you! Amen!"

Remember, explaining the salvation story in a way your child can grasp is crucial, as it helps them understand the significance of their decision and the love God has for them.

A Child of God I am, amen!

[Note to parent: Lead your child in prayer based on this topic].

TEACHING YOUR CHILDREN ABOUT THE TEN COMMANDMENTS

As a parent, you may wonder why the Ten Commandments are still relevant today. These commandments, which can be found in Exodus 20:1–17 and Deuteronomy 5:4–21, hold great significance in understanding the Old Testament and Jesus' teachings. They reflect God's moral standards for how His people should conduct themselves. While memorizing these verses is encouraged, their language can be challenging for children to grasp. To make it easier, we've created a chart that shows the contrast between a more complex and straightforward version.

God's commandments act as a guide, helping us to avoid self-destructive behavior and live a life of blessings in our imperfect world. It's important for children and families to understand these principles for living. Like other Bible teachings, these commandments show how adhering to moral values can shield us from harm and minimize suffering. This lesson is especially important for young children to learn.

God's law leads us to Christ, who is the prime example of flawlessly adhering to these divine rules. The commandments act as guides, showing children the challenges of living obediently and highlighting that only through Jesus can we attain a rightful relationship with our Creator. This journey transcends moral goodness; it's about preparing our hearts to repent and embrace Christ. This is the essence of teaching children about the Bible's teachings.

When explaining the Ten Commandments to your child, you can say that God wanted to help people live in a good way, so He gave them some rules. He asked Moses to climb up Mt. Sinai, where God gave him ten important rules called the Ten Commandments. The first four rules are about being close to God and reminding us to put God first, not worship anything else, never say God's name in a mean way, and take a special day to rest. The other six rules are about how to treat other people nicely and remind us not to tell lies, take things that aren't ours, be jealous of what others have, or hurt anyone.

God didn't give these rules to be bossy or mean. He gave them to help us live better lives. Even Jesus talked about these rules and reminded people that they aren't just for memorizing; they teach us how to love God and everyone around us. These rules are still true and helpful for us today.

THE TEN COMMANDMENTS FOR KIDS (PARAPHRASED)

	Ten Commandments (NIV) Exodus 20:1-17	10 Commandments for Kids (paraphrased in simple terms)
–	And God spoke all these words: I am the Lord your God, who brought you out of Egypt, out of the land of slavery.	Then God spoke all these words: I am the Lord your God. I brought you out of the land of Egypt where you were slaves.
1	You shall have no other gods before me.	Put God first.

2	You shall not make for yourself an image in the form of anything in heaven above or on the earth beneath or in the waters below. You shall not bow down to them or worship them.	Do not make fake gods.
3	You shall not misuse the name of the LORD your God, for the Lord will not hold anyone guiltless who misuses His name.	Respect God's name.
4	Remember the Sabbath day by keeping it holy.	Respect God's day of rest.
5	Honor your father and your mother, so that you may live long in the land the LORD your God is giving you.	Respect your parents.
6	You shall not murder.	Do not kill people.
7	You shall not commit adultery.	Respect marriage promises.
8	You shall not steal.	Do not steal.
9	You shall not give false testimony against your neighbor.	Do not lie.
10	You shall not covet your neighbor's house, spouse, servant, assets or anything that belongs to your neighbor.	Do not be jealous.

CHILDREN TRUST IN GOD'S HOLY WORD

In lands of tales where dreams take flight, a story shines with a guiding light.

It speaks of trust in whispers heard, in God's own Word, like songs of birds.

In pages filled with wondrous tales, a promise blooms, never frail.

It tells of love and journeys grand; in God's own Word, we firmly stand.

With Noah's ark and colors bright, a covenant in skies of light.

In every drop of rain that falls, God's Word within our hearts enthralls.

In deserts vast, a path was made, for Moses and his people's aid.

With staff in hand and faith so pure, God's Word their guide, forever sure.

In Bethlehem, a humble birth, a Savior came to heal the earth.

A story told of love so deep, in God's Word, our souls do leap.

Though tales of old, they may unfold, the truth within forever gold.

In every line and verse we've heard, Children, trust in God's Holy Word.

So let your hearts be open wide, in God's embrace, forever bide.

For through the pages, love is heard, Children, trust in God's Holy Word.

SCRIPTURES TO PRAY OVER YOUR CHILDREN - DAILY

Psalm 91:11 (NIV)

For He shall give His angels charge over you, to keep you in all your ways.

Numbers 6:24-26 (NIV)

The Lord bless you and protect you; The Lord make his face to shine upon you, and be gracious to you; The Lord lift up his countenance upon you and give you peace.

Psalm 139:14 (NIV)

I praise you because I am fearfully and wonderfully made; Your works are wonderful; I know that full[y] well.

Deuteronomy 31:6 (ICB)

Be strong and brave. Don't be afraid of them. Don't be frightened. The Lord your God will go with you. He will not leave you or forget you."

CHILDREN ARE MIGHTY ARROWS

(Psalms 127:4)

In meadows green, where sunshine plays like arrows bright on joyful days,

Children are treasures, pure and true, a gift of love, for me and you.

As Psalms do sing, in verse four, clear, like arrows swift, they bring us cheer,

Happy are parents, hearts so light, with a quiver full, their lives take flight.

With giggles, sweet and curious eyes, they fill our world with sweet surprise,

Like arrows aimed at destiny's call, in their laughter, we find our all.

Oh, children are arrows, strong and free, guiding us toward what we're meant to be.

A quiver full, a joyful song, in their embrace, we all belong.

So, let's embrace each tender smile, for they make our lives so worthwhile.

In Psalms, we find a truth so sweet, children are arrows, our hearts complete.

Happy are parents, so full of glee, blessed with a quiver, from one to three.

In their love and laughter, we thrive, with children like arrows, we truly come alive.

ABOUT THE AUTHOR

Pam Reece is a highly accomplished individual, known as a 4x bestselling author, radio and podcast show host, editor-in-chief of The BAM Magazine, mentor, speaker, and serial entrepreneur. With an impressive track record, Pam has been featured on numerous radio shows and magazines, including Kishma George's iWorship96 FM, Kishma George Radio Show/Acts Radio London, Blossoms of My Life, KKMC 880am, God's GEMS, La-Boo Publishing, Transcending Horizons, Creating Your Seat at The Table, Gospel Connection International Radio, Emergence Talk Radio, Bruised but not Broken, Dreams Come True, KISH Magazine, QUEEN Magazine, Headline News, Up Words, and more. She has also made multiple appearances on the Dreamer in You Show hosted by Dr. Kishma George on the Dominion.TV network and Atlanta Live WATC 57.

Pam Reece is the esteemed host of the highly successful Bust A Move Radio Show, a Christ-centered talk show that airs every Thursday night at 7 pm ET on EnvisionedBroadcasting.com. The show delves into a wide range of topics, including health, wealth, social issues, the Great Commission, empowerment, motivation, purpose, destiny, and more. With an impressive roster of guests, the show has featured entrepreneurs, celebrities, authors, social activists, recording artists, corporate professionals, apostles, prophets, pastors, teachers, relationship experts, financial experts, and gurus. The show's broadcasts reach and touch thousands of people across several continents, including Asia, Africa, North America, and Europe, with more than 25,000 podcast downloads on ten major podcast platforms.

In addition to her radio show, Pam Reece serves as the Editor-in-Chief of THE BAM Magazine, a highly regarded publication that launched successfully in 2022. This magazine shines a spotlight on phenomenal women and men who are making a global impact. Its featured contributors hail from various countries, including the USA, United Kingdom, Ghana, Nigeria, South Africa, and Zambia. The magazine also includes a kid's section and offers captivating reads on finance, information/technology, health/wellness, and relationships.

Professionally, Pam holds an undergraduate degree in business administration and paralegal studies. She has accumulated over 30 years of corporate America experience, working with Fortune 500 companies, small and medium-sized firms, as well as startups, in diverse industries such as law & regulatory affairs, human resources, business operations, corporate communications, biotech, software and technology, and employee events.

Pam Reece draws strength from her deep faith, believing in God's love, mercy, and grace. She understands her identity in Christ and embraces the truth that she is God's workmanship, created for good works that He prepared in advance for her to walk in. She lives by the principle that as long as one has a heartbeat, God has a plan. Pam emphasizes the importance of knowing oneself to make sound decisions and choose the right partnerships. She believes that a spirit of excellence, dignity, professionalism, and unwavering faith in God opens doors to spaces and opportunities unmatched by any other qualification. Pam's greatest joy is impacting as many lives as possible, offering hope, significance, and the motivation to fulfill God-ordained destinies.

Connect with Pam Reece:

Facebook: pamelareecemotivates, authorpamelareece, thebammagazine

Instagram: @palreece, @bustamovewithpamreece, @thebammagazine

Websites: www.pamelainternational.com; www.thebammagazine.com

Email: pamreecemotivates@gmail.com

www.ingramcontent.com/pod-product-compliance
Lightning Source LLC
Chambersburg PA
CBHW051812050726
47598CB00006B/2520